Pearls before swine

FINANCIAL WISDOM from the PAST...

IGNORED in the PRESENT

CONTENTS

FOREWORD

Swine? *Really?!?*

When I selected the title for this book, I knew I was running the risk of offending potential readers, which is typically not a good sales technique.

As a resident of the present, I'm not in a position to pass judgment on my contemporaries. I lack the proper perspective to compare current generations with those of the Age of Enlightenment or the Roman Empire. I am also guilty of many of the indictments that could be made of my fellow citizens. I have more house than I need (with a mortgage to match); I should save more than I do; I sometimes work too hard and other times I don't work hard enough; I don't practice delayed gratification very well; I want more than I'm willing to pay for; I have an inflated opinion of my own worth; I undervalue the opinions of others; I give money more thought than respect. My list of shortcomings is longer than this sampling.

As a lover of history, I am always interested in how past societies would view the way people behave in the twenty-first century. As a Financial Planner by profession, I am especially interested in how people from the past might view our actions and attitudes about money, in all its aspects and mutations.

One reason for my interest is the many paradoxes that people in the twenty-first century have created for themselves when it comes to money. We think about money more than any previous culture, yet our knowledge about money is inadequate and our wisdom about money is pathetic.

We have the ability to save and invest in well-regulated markets and institutions, yet we don't take proper advantage of them.

We spend thousands upon thousands of dollars educating each of our children. Our children invest twelve to twenty years of their own lives in formal education. We sacrifice so our children can get good jobs, which is necessary to make good money. But nowhere along the way do we stop and teach them anything useful about money.

We have the freedom to choose almost any career we want, yet we gravitate to whatever pays the most and/or requires the least. Such compromises assure that we will never have great success in our careers and will want to retire from them as soon as possible.

We can pay for our basic needs (food, clothing, shelter, transportation, and medical) with fewer hours of work than at any time in history, yet we run up record amounts of personal debt pursuing what we merely want, not what we truly need.

We allow our governments to generate so much debt that their very integrity is at risk because we are as yet unwilling to receive less from and/or pay more to these governments to keep them solvent.

We spend more time planning a vacation to Disney World than we do planning our family's finances for the year.

We pay for the prestige of certain brands, even

when we know there is no discernible difference in their quality compared to non-prestige brands. In the case of expensive items like cars, these purchases are usually made with borrowed funds.

We have the ability to be the healthiest creatures to ever walk the earth, but we choose to damage our health through poor diet, substance abuse, and inactivity. Then when we lose our health, we don't want to pay the high cost of getting well.

We can insure against most financial losses at a reasonable cost, yet we divert our capital to more pleasurable pursuits instead.

We have qualified advisors at our disposal through many media, plus the collective wisdom of centuries of mankind, yet we seek only what we want to hear, not what we need to hear.

It can be hard for us to recognize these self-made paradoxes because, when everyone is doing the same thing, we tend to think it is normal behavior. It takes the perspective of a different peer group to make us more fully aware of the folly of many of our financial habits.

What would Confucius, the Chinese philosopher who lived five hundred years before Christ, think about our inability to live within our means?

What would Virgil, the Roman poet from the time of Christ, think about our domination by fear and greed in the markets?

What would Benjamin Franklin, one of history's wisest and most prolific men on financial matters, think about our reluctance to plan for our future?

What would Abraham Lincoln, our 16th President, think of our attempts to receive more while working less?

What would Thoreau, Einstein, Socrates, Gandhi, Jesus, and others have to say about our misunderstandings about the role of money, wealth, possessions, and work in our lives?

The following pages contain the words of more than two-hundred individuals, spanning more than twenty-five centuries. Their purpose here is to give us a better sense of where we are today in a world that runs on money and to provide guidance and inspiration to help us become better stewards of what has been entrusted to us.

The average American today lives far better than the richest king of just a couple of centuries ago. Despite our material comfort, we do not seem happy with our lot. We worry constantly about money, even though we are the most comfortable humans in history. If these great figures from the past could reappear today and observe us firsthand, I do not think we would receive a glowing evaluation. They might view their words of wisdom as pearls cast before swine. It's not too late to prove them wrong.

THE OMNIPRESENT ABSTRACTION

Before beginning any conversation about money, we should have some idea what we're talking about.

To get an indication of just how deeply money is integrated into our lives, digest the following:

I, (Name), Take you, (Name),
To be my (wife/husband);
To have and to hold,
From this day forward,
For better, for worse,
For richer, for poorer,
In sickness and in health,
To love and to cherish,
Till death do us part.

Traditional Wedding Vows

This wedding vow is the most solemn pledge that most people make in their lives, and some eighty-five percent of the population makes this pledge at least once in their lives.

Right there in the middle of these vows is the promise that we will remain married regardless of our financial condition in the future. We promise that we will remain together for better or worse, which is affected in no small part by our financial condition. We also promise to remain together in sickness and in health. There is a positive correlation between wealth and health, and comparatively few marriages break up because a spouse becomes ill.

These traditional wedding vows date back to at least 1549, when they were first published in the prayer book for the Church of England. Clearly, the danger to marriages posed by financial calamity or carelessness is not a new phenomenon.

Financial problems are often cited as a leading cause of divorce. Divorced couples cite financial problems as the cause of divorce more often than do professional counselors. This discrepancy is because while most divorcing couples think that money problems are the cause, professional counselors can see that money problems are often a manifestation of other, more serious problems in a marriage.

For a man-made instrument with no intrinsic value, money sure kicks up a lot of dust.

> *That money is where most of us are tested says precisely as much about the weakness of man as it does about the power of money.*
>
> Jacob Needleman (1934-)
> Author, Philosopher

For better or worse, money has become our principal means of contact with the outside world. Think about all the contacts you have with people in a typical month. How many of them involve money as the main reason for the contact? Every business transaction would be included in this category. How many of these monthly contacts have some monetary aspect to them? Even organizations you belong to, such as a church or social club, have dues or financial pledges. Even such organizations that are not created for a business purpose will have a financial obligation as a condition for membership. There is a paid admission.

Even marriage, which should involve more love and less money than any other relationship, has a financial component from the beginning. The payment of a dowry is a four-thousand-year-old practice of the wife providing financial assets to begin the marriage. One of its main purposes is to protect the wife against ill treatment by the husband or his family. The dowry system is still practiced in parts of south Asia.

Modern western marriages begin with a major financial component, too - the engagement ring. The ring is supposed to symbolize the commitment of the partners, though it also has come to symbolize the financial strength of the groom-to-be. In the early twentieth century, DeBeers began suggesting that three months' wages was an appropriate amount to spend on an engagement ring. The average amount spent on an engagement ring today exceeds $2,000, which isn't close to three month's wages for the typical groom-to-be. While an engagement ring can be a major investment, at least it's encouraging that people aren't blindly following the guidelines set by the world's largest producer of diamonds.

> *Money is a new form of slavery, which differs from the old only in being impersonal, and in freeing people from all the human relations of the slave.*
>
> Leo Tolstoy (1828-1910)
> Russian Novelist

In this world, we have **social norms** and **market norms.** Social norms involve the interactions between humans. They are about helping each other and getting along. They are the glue that holds a society together. They are biological. Market norms involve a bottom line. They are transaction-based. They can be precisely measured. They are mechanical.

The first thing to realize is that when social norms collide with market norms, social norms lose. This collision almost always occurs when market norms invade the world of social norms. For example, how many budding romantic relationships have come to a screeching halt because at some point the guy brought up how much he had spent on dates and that he wasn't "getting anything in return?" That one comment shifted the relationship from social norms to market norms. In such a developing relationship, it also shifted the dynamic from pleasure to business. Nothing kills a relationship faster than shifting it from pleasure to business prematurely.

In business relationships, market norms should rule. In social relationships, social norms should rule. When you are invited to a friend's house for dinner, you bring a nice bottle of wine as a gift; you don't offer to "pay the tab" at the end of the evening. When your neighbor asks to borrow your chain saw, you lend it with the expectation he will return the favor in the future; you don't charge him rent.

If you introduce market norms where social norms prevail, market norms will win. But know that social norms may never return and that they never forget, either.

Riches should be admitted into our houses, but not into our hearts; we may take them into our possession, but not into our affections.

Pierre Charron (1541-1603)
French Philosopher

A wise man should have money in his head, but not in his heart.

Jonathan Swift (1667-1745)
English Novelist

You should always love people and use money, rather than the reverse.

Bob Proctor (1940-)
Motivational Speaker

One of the primary reasons money seems to dominate so much of our lives is because we have allowed ourselves to become emotionally attached to it. We have allowed it to invade our hearts.

Our material and economic needs are important, but they were never meant to be more important than our spiritual needs. Ours is one of the first societies that has encouraged people to be self-sufficient and autonomous. We admire "rugged individualism." The problem with such autonomy, which is made possible with money more than anything else, is that it can lead to a disconnect between the individual and the rest of society, as well as a disconnect between the individual and that person's spiritual side.

> *Money is not required to buy one necessity of the soul.*
> Henry David Thoreau (1817-1862)
> Author, Philosopher

There is a certain paradox to America. We have a very high standard of living, while at the same time we have a very high religious affiliation. No other country has a combined score in spirituality and materialism that is as high. Our collective faith, at least when measured by levels of participation in organized religious services, seems to keep us grounded enough that materialism doesn't totally consume us as a nation.

> *Prosperity is only an instrument to be used, not a deity to be worshipped.*
> Calvin Coolidge (1872-1933)
> 30th U.S. President
>
> *Money is only a tool. It will take you wherever you wish, but it will not replace you as the driver.*
> Ayn Rand (1905-1982)
> Novelist, Philosopher

When money becomes desired for what it is, rather than for what it can do, it is worse than someone who collects classic automobiles but never drives them. It seems a waste to just let a classic car sit, but it can still be admired for its styling. Money has no styling. You can't display it in a museum and charge admission. Unless money is serving some purpose, the possession of it and the effort made to acquire and possess it is a waste.

Money is like love; it kills slowly and painfully the one who withholds it, and enlivens the other who turns it upon his fellow man.

Kahlil Gibran (1883-1931)
Poet, Philosopher

Money is like manure. You have to spread it around or it smells.

J. Paul Getty (1892-1976)
Founder, Getty Oil Company

Money that is not in circulation is useless, just as your blood is useless if it isn't in circulation through your veins and arteries.

I am not saying that money that isn't being spent isn't in circulation. Too many people and too many governments have been putting too much money into circulation, often borrowing the money from future generations. They have not saved and invested enough of the money that has crossed their palms.

Saving and investing does not take money out of circulation. It provides capital for the creation of more money in the future. Adequate savings and investments provide economic security for their owners, which is one of the most important tasks that money is asked to perform.

When the accumulation of money goes well past the point of what is necessary to maintain economic security, the efficient use of that money can become compromised. More important, the time and energy its owner expends in the accumulation of ever more money is inefficient. They trade ever-dwindling resources for a resource they don't need at all.

> *Riches are a good handmaid, but the worst mistress.*
>
> Sir Francis Bacon (1561-1626)
> English Philosopher, Statesman
>
> *Money frees you from doing things you dislike. Since I dislike doing nearly everything, money is handy.*
>
> Groucho Marx (1890-1977)
> Comedian

Money is history's greatest labor-saving device. Money enables work to be assigned to others who can do it more efficiently than you can. This process of assignment frees up your time to be used more efficiently.

When the accumulation and protection of money (and those things that money can buy) begins to consume more and more of one's time and energy, money ceases to be a labor-saving device and becomes a labor-making device for its owner. In such circumstances, the owner of money becomes possessed by the possession.

Money is not exempt from the **law of marginal utility**, which states that the more we have of something, the less we value each additional unit.

Individuals have to determine when they have reached a point where the effort to have more is not worth the more they will have.

> *The gratification of wealth is not found in mere possession or in lavish expenditure, but in its wise application.*
>
> Miguel de Cervantes (1547-1616)
> Spanish Novelist, Poet
>
> *A man who both spends and saves money is the happiest man, because he has both enjoyments.*
>
> Samuel Johnson (1709-1784)
> English Poet, Essayist

A true craftsman would much rather show you the products he has made, than show you the tools with which he made them. It should be the same way with money.

We all have this same tendency, to varying degrees. Some people will use their money to buy items that clearly show how much money they spent, and by extension, how much money they have. Think about cars that cost upwards of six figures. There is no practical reason for someone to spend so much for a car. Certain makes and models of cars tell the world in no uncertain terms that its owner has some serious financial means. There is a long list of items that we can buy whose primary, if not sole purpose, is to tell the world just how much we are worth in dollars and cents.

The true craftsman works his tools to create items that have both utility and beauty. A true craftsman with money should do the same thing. While there is nothing wrong with the occasional self-indulgent extravagance, if the majority of one's money is used for such a purpose, that can hardly be considered a wise application. A person's money should be allocated among sharing, saving, and spending. The amount allocated to each category will vary from person to person, but it is important that the stated order of priority be followed. When spending comes first, sharing and saving will always receive less than their due.

> *If your only goal is to become rich, you will never achieve it.*
>
> John D. Rockefeller (1839-1937)
> Founder, Standard Oil Company

Becoming rich is a dream, if not a goal, for many of us. However, most people who become rich do so as a by-product of a different goal, which can be described generally as providing a needed product or service to as many people as possible. Becoming rich was the effect, not the cause.

"Becoming rich" is also a vague term. When we want to lose weight, we don't say we want to "become thin," because thin is a vague term that is subject to interpretation and is hard to measure. We will instead state a goal of reaching a target weight, then work toward that goal. Once we reach our target weight, we rarely continue losing weight just to see how thin we can become.

Even if someone sets a wealth goal (a net worth

of $1 million, $5 million, $100 million), that person is never satisfied once that goal is achieved. One of the characteristics of money is that it is addictive. The man who thought he would be happy with a net worth of $1 million will find himself working harder than ever when his net worth is $100 million. Making money can be like drinking sea water; it doesn't quench the thirst; it only increases it.

> *For the love of money is a root of all kinds of evil. Some people, eager for money, have wandered from the faith and pierced themselves with many griefs.*
>
> 1 Timothy 6:7-10
>
> *So you think that money is the root of all evil? Have you ever asked what the root of money is? Money is made possible only by those who produce. Is this what you consider evil?*
>
> Ayn Rand (1905-1982)
> Novelist, Philosopher

It's important to remember that the Biblical passage does not say that **money** is the root of all evil; it says that the **love** of money is the root of all evil.

It isn't money's fault that so many problems stem from its use, misuse, and abuse. Money is inert. It has no personality, no agenda, and it plays no favorites. The only problem with money is all the stupid things humans concoct to do with it. When people and money come together, it is important to remember that, of the two, only people are inherently flawed.

Any tool is subject to misuse. Anyone who has ever been hit on the head with a frying pan or seen *The Texas Chainsaw Massacre* knows what I mean. Money, as we think of it, was started by King Croesus of Lydia over 2,500 years ago to facilitate trade. Croesus would be stunned to see how important money is in the modern world. He would also be stunned to see how creative we've become in finding new ways to abuse money.

> *If a man has money, it is usually a sign too, that he knows how to take care of it. Don't imagine his money is easy to get simply because he has plenty of it.*
>
> Edgar Watson Howe (1853-1937)
> Novelist, Editor
>
> *Those who obtain riches by labor, care, and watching know their value. Those who impart them to sustain and extend knowledge, virtue, and religion know their use. Those who lose them by accident or fraud know their vanity. And those who experience the difficulties and dangers of preserving them know their perplexities.*
>
> Charles Simmons (1893-1975)
> Member, British Parliament

Considering how much time we spend in the pursuit of money, we spend remarkably little time in trying to understand money. I'm not referring here to spending time learning how to make money; I'm talking about understanding the ways money affects individuals and societies.

Because we rarely take any serious time to look at how money can affect us, we end up unprepared for the changes that money can bring. If the people who play the lottery listened to the stories of past winners and the problems that sudden wealth caused them, many would reconsider spending good money on those tickets.

Money is not to be taken lightly because of the effects, both positive and negative, that it can have on all those who are touched by it. Only those who seriously attempt to understand money can hope to control it, rather than be controlled by it.

Men, such as they are, very naturally seek money or power; and power because it is as good as money.
Ralph Waldo Emerson (1803-1882)
Philosopher, Essayist

The men who can manage men manage the men who manage only things.
The men who can manage money manage all.
Will Durant (1885-1981)
Historian, Philosopher

Between money and power, I believe money is the more desirable. Power is only power, but money can buy power, and almost everything else, too. The Colt revolver was called the Great Equalizer in the Wild West. Money has similar powers in the modern world. Money has the ability to make unequals seem equal and to make equals seem unequal.

Almost everyone gives greater deference and latitude to someone if we think that person has money. We can see it even in the halls of justice, where everyone is presumed to be equal. Recall the revised definition of capital punishment - those who have the capital don't get the punishment.

Money buys preferred treatment in the more mundane tasks of life, too. Those of us who fly coach must suffer the indignity of walking past our fellow travellers who are already comfortably ensconced in first class. Studies have shown that drivers wait longer to honk at someone who fails to proceed at a green light if that person is driving an expensive car.

I am opposed to millionaires, but it would be dangerous to offer me the position.

Mark Twain (1835-1910)
Author, Humorist

To suppose as we all suppose, that we could be rich and not behave as the rich behave, is like supposing that we could drink all day and stay sober.

Logan Pearsall Smith (1865-1946)
Essayist

A rich man is nothing but a poor man with money.

W.C. Fields (1880-1946)
Comedian, Actor

One luxury the rich don't have that the rest of the population enjoys is the opportunity to mock the rich. Many a movie and television show has poked fun at the supposed ways of the rich, from the inanity of Thurston Howell III on *Gilligan's Island* to the sadistic greediness of Carter Pewterschmidt on *Family Guy*.

Part of the reason for such negative stereotypes

is ignorance on who the rich really are. The best-selling book *The Millionaire Next Door* revealed that most millionaires are little different from the general population. Most are first-generation rich and earned their fortunes by starting businesses that the author refers to as "dull-normal."

> *The best way to realize the pleasure of feeling rich is to live in a smaller house than your means would entitle you to have.*
>
> Edward Clarke (1841-1931)
> British Solicitor-General

One of the most important factors cited in how millionaires become millionaires is their belief that financial independence is more important than displaying high social status. That core principle is the inspiration for the book's title. That principle also means there are two truths about millionaires that most people have wrong. The first truth is that most of the millionaires out there are camouflaged, living well below their means in modest, but comfortable, homes and driving sensible cars.

The second truth is that many of the people we think are millionaires are probably faking it. The social status that is to be gained by appearing to be rich is so tempting that many people put themselves into financial ruin by trying to maintain such appearances. The more opulent the lifestyle, the greater the chance that it will all collapse like a house of credit cards.

Poor men seek meat for their stomachs.
Rich men seek stomachs for their meat.

English Proverb

If any man is rich and powerful he comes under the law of God by which the higher branches must take the burning of the sun, and shade those that are lower; the tall trees must protect the weak plants beneath them.

Henry Ward Beecher (1813-1887)
Clergyman, Abolitionist

No one would remember the Good Samaritan if he'd only had good intentions. He had money, too.

Margaret Thatcher (1925-   )
British Prime Minister

Wealth is created by producing more than you consume. Poverty is created by consuming more than you produce. This axiom is true for both nations and individuals.

Before rich men seek stomachs for their meat, they first make sure their own stomachs are full. They recognize that the best way to keep their own stomachs full is to fill other stomachs, for a price.

Wealth is created by creating something of value to others, something for which others are willing to pay. It is certainly easier to create something of value to others, and to create wealth in the process, when you are well-fed, well-educated, and well-capitalized. When you are spending most of your waking hours seeking meat for your stomach, creating something of value to others doesn't even enter into your head.

When thinking about creating something of value

for others, the most valuable creation is the opportunity for others to create value for others, and thus, in time, create wealth for themselves.

> *This is one of the bitter curses of poverty: it leaves no right to be generous.*
>
> George Gissing (1857-1903)
> English Novelist
>
> *There is only one class in the community that thinks more about money than the rich, and that is the poor. The poor can think of nothing else. That is the misery of being poor.*
>
> Oscar Wilde (1854-1900)
> Irish Writer, Poet

When the rich think about becoming richer, they tend to think in terms of new products or services they can provide, as well as more efficient ways of providing current goods or services. When the poor think of becoming rich, they do not tend to think in terms of new products or services they can provide. For most of them, they do not possess the skills or the capital to provide products or services of value to others. The poor think of becoming rich through long shots, like winning the lottery, which does not create wealth, but merely transfers it. Counting on a long shot to end one's poverty merely deepens the poverty with every scheme that fails.

In a country well governed, poverty is something to be ashamed of. In a country badly governed, wealth is something to be ashamed of.

Confucius (551-479 BC)
Chinese Philosopher

A decent provision for the poor is the true test of civilization.

Samuel Johnson (1709-1784)
English Poet, Essayist

The worst country to be poor in is America.

Arnold Toynbee (1889-1975)
English Historian

Because we in America believe our form of government to be the best that mankind has yet devised, we feel the need to act when we see poverty in our midst. However, poverty is a **result** of a lack of money; it is not a **symptom** of a lack of money. Poverty is a symptom of a lack of production. A person in poverty is not producing anything anyone wants to buy, at least not in sufficient quantities to provide an adequate income. The reasons for a person's lack of production can run the gamut from severe birth defects to just plain laziness.

I'm not convinced that there are a lot of lazy people in poverty, for the simple reason that poverty has a way of beating the laziness out of all but the worst sloths. The worst sloths are the ones who simply **won't** be productive, regardless of the consequences.

I'm also not convinced that there are huge

numbers of Americans who **can't** be productive. The percentage of people in poverty who, because of a physical or mental handicap, can't do anything is fairly small. (I consider the elderly in a separate category, as most were productive when they were younger.) These people are the poor that Jesus said would always be with us. These people are the poor that have no hope of lifting themselves out of poverty. These people are the poor that should cause us shame should we choose to ignore them.

> *A lean purse is easier to cure than endure.*
>
> George Clason (1874-1957)
> Businessman

The majority of those in poverty have the desire and the ability to work their way out of poverty, if they are given the opportunity. They actually prefer a hand up to a handout. The challenge is to teach them how to create wealth for themselves.

We respect most the money we earn through our own hard labors. The respect for that money is merely an extension of the respect we have for ourselves for earning that money through our own hard labors. When people are not given the opportunity to be self-supporting, the opportunity to earn that self-respect is denied. Well-intentioned programs that bestow what can and should be earned disserve those it means to serve.

The Ten Cannots:

- *You cannot bring about prosperity by discouraging thrift.*
- *You cannot strengthen the weak by weakening the strong.*
- *You cannot help little men by tearing down big men.*
- *You cannot lift the wage earner by pulling down the wage payer.*
- *You cannot help the poor by destroying the rich.*
- *You cannot establish sound security on borrowed money.*
- *You cannot further the brotherhood of man by inciting class hatred.*
- *You cannot keep out of trouble by spending more than you earn.*
- *You cannot build character and courage by destroying men's initiative & independence.*
- *And you cannot help men permanently by doing for them what they can and should do for themselves.*

William Boetcker (1873-1962)
Presbyterian Minister

When the rich and the poor think about each other, two stereotypes seem to emerge. The rich give in to the stereotype that the poor **will not** work to obtain wealth. The poor give in to the stereotype that the rich **did not** work to obtain wealth. While there are examples of the stereotype in both groups, the vast majority in both groups do not fit the stereotype at all.

> *That some should be rich shows that others may become rich and, hence, is just encouragement to industry and enterprise. Let not him who is houseless pull down the house of another, but let him labor diligently and build one for himself, thus, by example, assuring that his own shall be safe from violence when built.*
>
> Abraham Lincoln (1809-1965)
> 16th U.S. President
>
> *Those who condemn wealth are those who have none and see no chance of getting it.*
>
> William Penn Patrick (1930-1973)
> Entrepreneur

As long as someone without money sees the possibility of obtaining money, that person is not likely to favor radical redistribution of wealth. Such redistribution serves as a disincentive for wealth creation, to those who are currently producing wealth, and also to those who hope to be producing it in the future. No one wants to learn new disciplines and make new sacrifices if the gains to be made from those sacrifices can't be retained.

> *Wealth is not a pizza. If I have too many slices, you don't have to eat the Domino's box.*
>
> P.J. O'Rourke (1947-)
> Satirist, Journalist

Wealth is a resource. When we think about resources, we tend to think about natural resources, like gold or oil. Those kinds of resources are finite.

When we consume a unit of that resource, it is gone forever. If a finite resource is hoarded or wasted, others can be adversely affected. When it comes to a finite resource that everyone wants, disputes over ownership and fairness of distribution can lead to wars, between classes as well as countries.

Wealth is a resource, but it is hardly finite. The people who create wealth are at least as valuable a resource as the wealth they create. Wealth as a resource is like knowledge, not oil. An increase in my knowledge doesn't make everyone else dumber, and an increase in my wealth doesn't make everyone else poorer.

In 1950, the economies of Afghanistan and South Korea were approximately the same size. Today the economy of South Korea is fifty times the size of Afghanistan's. South Korea's only natural resource is its people. They have created wealth by creating knowledge among its people. They maintain that wealth through hard work and thrift. South Korea has created wealth as a nation in the same way individuals create wealth, by understanding that wealth is created primarily with an unlimited resource that all humans possess to some degree.

A great fortune is a great slavery.

Seneca (54 BC - 39 AD)
Roman Statesman

God must love the rich or he wouldn't divide so much among so few of them.

H.L. Mencken (1880-1956)
Essayist, Satirist

While no one aspires to be poor, it's important to remember that there are drawbacks to being wealthy, too. Even those who are not rich know that the more you possess, the more your possessions may possess you. Think about something as simple as owning a second car. The utility and/or pleasure of owning that second car may be more than offset by the effort required to maintain it. Everything we own makes demands of us, and when we own a lot of something, even money, what we get in return may not be worth what we sacrifice to own it.

Worldly riches are like nuts; many clothes are torn getting them, many a tooth broke in cracking them, but never a belly full in eating them.

Ralph Venning (1621-1674)
English Clergyman

Anyone who works with tools for a living knows that it's important to keep the tools of one's trade in good working condition. These tools enable the job to be done, and to be done in a more efficient manner. However, a tool must be used often enough and efficiently enough to justify its cost and its upkeep. It makes no sense to have a shop full of tools that don't offset the cost in time, effort, and money to own them by generating wealth through the production of goods or services.

Money is a tool, too. Because money is precise, we know when the monetary cost exceeds the monetary benefit. We rarely know with any accuracy when the intangible costs of maintaining wealth exceed the benefits of that wealth. We usually become aware of these "hidden costs" only after they exact an exorbitant price.

> *No amount of money is worth the sacrifice of one's better instincts, of one's self-respect – of one's soul, if you wish. Riches not gained legitimately and decently are not worth having.*
>
> B.C. Forbes (1880-1954)
> Founder, Forbes Magazine

Like any tool, money in the right hands used for the right purpose can greatly benefit all whom it touches. And, like any tool, money in the wrong hands used for the wrong purpose can bring great destruction.

Once someone has had money for a time, money's limitations become evident. Also, as we get older and realize our own limitations (especially the limitation of time), we begin to think less of how our money might benefit us and more of how it might benefit others. It is at this point in one's life that a philanthropist is born.

> *Today, the world knows the poetry of Shakespeare, the music of Wagner, the art of Rembrandt; but who knows even the names of the money barons of their day – or cares to know? If you want your name to live after you, you'll not give all your thought to money.*
>
> Edwin Baird (1886-1957)
> Publisher

Too many people spend too many years working too hard to get money. They expend their health to obtain wealth, only to then spend their wealth to regain their health. It isn't just the time and effort we sacrifice that is the price of wealth. The bigger price comes in the long-term damage to our physical, mental, and spiritual health.

> *The first wealth is health.*
>
> Ralph Waldo Emerson (1803-1882)
> Philosopher, Essayist
>
> *I don't like money actually, but it quiets my nerves.*
>
> Joe Louis (1914-1981)
> World Boxing Champion

The great majority of the workforce takes jobs that offer little more than the biggest paycheck. People work such jobs like they're a prison sentence, counting the days until they can retire. Often, the stress of working a job that's a misfit causes health problems that force a premature retirement or damages the quality of retirement. Working a job that is fun and fulfilling is much healthier, even if it pays less and requires a few more years in the workforce. I would personally rather work forty years at a job I love than thirty years at one I hate.

Despite the fact that a large number of people stress themselves out in the pursuit of wealth, it is better for your health to be rich than poor. Like everything else in life, the trick is to find a proper balance between what you want and what you are willing to sacrifice to get it.

> *I am indeed rich, since my income is superior to my expense, and my expense is equal to my wishes.*
>
> Edward Gibson (1837-1913)
> Lord Chancellor of Ireland
>
> *You are financially secure when you can afford anything you want and you don't want anything.*
>
> Art Buchwald (1925-2007)
> Author, Journalist

Most of the money problems people have are less the result of too little money and more the result of too much desire. Few of us have the ability to control our incomes - we all have the ability to control our desires. As such, it makes sense to control what we have the ability to control.

Controlling the desire for material goods is not easy in a country where credit is easy to obtain and we also receive nearly three-thousand marketing messages every day. Both the credit pitch and the marketing pitch are designed to create desire, and desire involves things we want, not things we need.

When we first attend to the financial items we need (savings, insurance, 401k, etc.), we greatly reduce the risk that we will run into financial problems. People who live at a poverty level are unlikely to be able to fund all their financial needs. If they can't afford health insurance, it isn't usually because they bought a new car instead. Placing wants over needs and putting one at financial risk is more common in the middle class, where credit is easier to obtain, where the pressure to keep up with the neighbors is stronger, and where there is greater optimism that earnings will increase and that everything will work out in the end.

> *Goods can serve many other purposes besides purchasing money, but money can serve no other purpose besides purchasing goods.*
>
> Adam Smith (1723-1790)
> Scottish Philosopher, Economist

There is a paradox to money, in that it is an instrument of precision that creates great distortions. We judge the importance and worth of other human beings based on how much money they earn. Because money is our most common denominator, we use it as the default measure of a person's worth.

There are hedge fund managers that have made as much in a year as twenty-thousand teachers combined. We want to think that we would treat the hedge fund manager and the teacher equally, but we know which one will get the media attention and the preferential treatment.

What's worse than judging others by their wealth and income is judging ourselves by that standard. We beat ourselves up because we don't have a bigger income, because we don't have a bigger stock portfolio, because we don't have a nicer home, a nicer car, or a nicer (fill-in-the-blank).

We all know someone who makes more money than we do, who is also a person of inferior character. We know that we are the better person in every human quality that matters. We have integrity that other person can't touch. And yet, we will still feel a sense of inferiority when we remember that we are the one with less money. We feel this way because the other person is using money to make everyone else feel inferior, and it's easy to submit to that mindset. Also, we defer to whatever method of comparison we can quantify. We can't measure one's integrity, but we can measure their net worth, so that becomes the basis of comparison.

> *If you want to know how rich you really are, find out what would be left of you tomorrow if you should lose every dollar you own tonight.*
>
> William Boetcker (1873-1962)
> Presbyterian Minister

Money is always with us - motivating us, goading us, measuring us, judging us. Money can wield great power over us, but only to the extent we let it.

INTERNAL IMPERFECTIONS

We spend most of our lives swimming against the currents of our own humanness.

In 1974, the Doobie Brothers released an album titled *What Were Once Vices Are Now Habits.* The album's title succinctly and accurately described what had been transpiring over the previous decade.

The period from the mid-'60's to the mid-'70's may have been the most socially upheaving period in American history. There were certainly many positive changes during that period, such as the passage of the Civil Rights Act and the moon landing. We also had assassinations, the Vietnam War, Watergate, urban riots, and the hippie movement, to name a few of the less stellar events of the period.

Behavior that was condemned by society in the early '60's was tolerated, condoned, and sometimes celebrated by the mid-'70's. Consider the aforementioned Doobie Brothers. **Doobie** is slang for marijuana joint. Can you imagine a group naming themselves the Doobie Brothers, getting signed by a record label and getting songs played on the radio in the early '60's, when the charts were dominated by artists like the Shirelles, Chubby Checker, Brenda Lee, and Fabian? *What Were*

Once Pariahs Are Now Rock Stars.

> *Many without punishment, none without sin.*
> John Ray (1627-1705)
> English Naturalist

In 1969, Diana Ross and the Supremes recorded a song titled "Love Child." The song was controversial at the time because it dealt directly with the subject of a (potential) unplanned and unwanted pregnancy. The singer urges her boyfriend to be patient about having sex. She was herself a "love child," born out of wedlock with no father around. She did not want her child to suffer the way she had suffered by growing up without a mother and father raising her together.

Fast forward to 1997, a generation later. B-Rock and the Bizz have their only hit, a song titled "My Baby Daddy." In the song, when the girl's current boyfriend asks about the man she has been seen with, her dismissive reply (repeated some fifty times) is "That's just my baby daddy."

> *It is a wise father that knows his own child.*
> William Shakespeare (1564-1616)
> English Playwright

In 1940, just 3.8% of U.S. births were to unmarried women. Today that figure is around 40%, a ten-fold increase over three generations. When "Love Child" was released, less than 25% of black children were born to unmarried mothers.

When "My Baby Daddy" was released, that figure had climbed to nearly 70%. It is unlikely that either song had a measurable effect on the out-of-wedlock birthrate. Their importance is as an indicator of the change in attitude over a generation.

The out-of-wedlock birthrate has also climbed in most of the industrialized world, with the exception of Japan, where the rate is only about 2%. Japan is a homogeneous population, where an individual's rights do not extend to the point where the individual can act in a way that creates a burden on the larger society. The social pressure not to create a child that the state may have to support is much greater in Japan than in the U.S.

> *One of the misfortunes of our time is that in getting rid of false shame we have killed off so much real shame as well.*
>
> Louis Kronenberger (1904-1980)
> Author, Drama Critic

Over the last four or five decades, we have become much less judgmental toward others. Such change is good when we have been judgmental about what a person is. Unfortunately, in our desire to be less judgmental about what a person **is,** we have abdicated our responsibility to be judgmental about what a person **does.**

When a society is no longer willing to do the difficult and sometimes unpleasant task of passing judgment on the actions of others, that society often justifies such inaction by reclassifying vices as habits.

Both vices and habits are what a person does; they are not what a person is. As such, they are subject to the judgment of society. A society has both the right and the responsibility to pass judgment on the actions of a person, when those actions have an adverse effect on the larger society.

> *The chains of habit are too weak to be felt until they are too strong to be broken.*
>
> Samuel Johnson (1709-1784)
> English Poet, Essayist

As a free society, we should pass judgment on vices, but not on habits. Most habits, such as poor hygiene, may not be applauded by society, but they do not offend to the point where taking action to curtail such a habit is warranted. Upgrading a vice to a habit relieves society of their responsibility to act in any meaningful way.

While we have become less judgmental about some actions that affect society, we have become more judgmental about some areas that affect society less. We no longer feel it is our right to pass judgment on someone producing children that will require state support, yet we are perfectly comfortable telling that same person that they may not smoke. Just as we have upgraded vices to habits to remove responsibility to judge them, we have downgraded some habits to vices to justify passing judgment on others.

> *What maintains one vice would bring up two children.*
> Benjamin Franklin (1706-1790)
> Founding Father

Whether someone's personal behavior is labeled a vice or a habit, the responsibility of society to pass judgment on that behavior begins when the society as a whole is adversely affected by it. A society can and should debate the moral and cultural effects of a vast array of human behavior, from smoking pot to viewing pornography.

When individual rights get measured against unquantifiable damages to society, the courts are likely to decide in favor of individual rights. To enable society to justify limiting individual rights, society must prove that a behavior causes a quantifiable damage to society. And the best way to quantify anything in society is with our old friend, money.

Prohibition was not repealed because it impinged on individual freedoms or because studies on alcohol consumption proved it wasn't harmful. Prohibition was repealed because it did not reduce alcohol consumption, and the money that used to go to legitimate businesses and to tax coffers was going instead to tax-evading criminal organizations.

The War on Drugs is now more than forty years old, and drug use in the U.S. is higher now than when that war began. This war is being re-evaluated, not because anyone thinks that drugs are good for society, but because after spending approximately one **trillion** dollars, there has been no discernible progress.

Prohibition and the War on Drugs are examples of efforts to restrict bad behavior that have failed by any financial measure. There are examples of efforts to restrict bad behavior that have succeeded, too. Stricter drunk driving and seat belt laws have reduced deaths and injuries from auto accidents. Such laws are defensible because the economic cost of injuries and death are not borne solely or even primarily by the person who drinks and drives or who doesn't wear a seat belt. Society is required to build more hospitals, hire more EMTs, increase the court docket, and pay higher insurance premiums.

> *If we don't discipline ourselves,*
> *the world will do it for us.*
>
> William Feather (1889-1981)
> Publisher, Author

Whether we are talking about an individual or a nation, they follow the same pattern when it comes to how their behavior is affected by their support system. For both, the larger and more anonymous the safety net, the more careless is their behavior.

Before the creation of the European Union and a common currency, individual countries in Europe bore the full brunt of their own fiscal mismanagement. When these countries decided to tie their economic fates together, it was inevitable that some of them would behave more recklessly, knowing they could count on their partners to rescue them. That rescue was assured because their ties meant that if one country drowned, they were all in danger of drowning.

The same behavior can be found all the way down to the family level. When there are parents, siblings, aunts, uncles, or cousins there to back up and bail out a member, there is a greater chance that someone in that family will behave in a manner that necessitates the backup or the bailout.

When the backup/bailout comes in the form of thousands or millions of anonymous taxpayers, the temptation to give in to one's vices increases dramatically. This behavior is hardly limited to the person who has a child out of wedlock, knowing that there will be public assistance to cover most of the expense of raising that child.

The financial meltdown of 2008 was largely precipitated by firms that knew they could privatize the profit but socialize the risk because they were "too big to fail." If their reckless behavior caused a problem, no matter how catastrophic, anyone and everyone who would be adversely affected would come to the rescue, if only to protect their own interests. The larger the parties to be adversely affected and the more numerous they were, the larger and stronger the safety net was for these firms. They were playing with house money.

> *If you do what you should not,*
> *you must bear what you would not.*
>
> Benjamin Franklin (1706-1790)
> Founding Father

We have become a society of enablers. An enabler is a third party that takes responsibility for, and makes accommodations for and assumes liabilities of another party's harmful conduct. The enabler's actions are intended to help, but only tend to perpetuate the problem. Addicts never seek treatment as long as there are enablers shielding them from the full force of the damage they are causing. Drugs and alcohol are not the only addictions, and they may be some of the milder ones. Individuals are addicted to entitlements paid for by others. Corporations are addicted to risk for a quick stock boost. Governments are addicted to debt to keep themselves in power. Only when individuals, corporations, and governments are required to bear the full brunt of their actions will they act responsibly.

> *Discipline without freedom is tyranny.*
> *Freedom without discipline is chaos.*
>
> Cullen Hightower (1923-)
> Writer

A refusal to accept responsibility for one's actions is an invitation to regulation by others. Chaos is too often solved through tyranny. Take something as common as driving your car. Your state requires you to have liability insurance to protect others before you can even drive your car. When you get in your car, you are required by law to buckle up. These regulations were put in place because too many people did not have insurance or wear their seat belts when it was voluntary, even though they were aware of the potential harm their actions could cause to themselves and others.

There are at least two problems with increased regulation. First, for every new regulation that is put in place, resources have to be devoted to enforcing that regulation. Those resources are siphoned from other areas that are almost always more productive. Second, the people the regulations are trying to control most are also the ones most likely to ignore the regulations. If a regulation is put in place because 10% of the population is engaging in a harmful behavior, that 10% will usually continue to engage in that same behavior. Meanwhile, the 90% who already behave appropriately will be burdened with proving their compliance.

> *It takes 20 years to build a reputation and five minutes to ruin it. If you think about that, you'll do things differently.*
>
> Warren Buffett (1930-)
> Investor, Philanthropist

A person's reputation is the collective opinion of everyone who has an opinion of that person. Only people who are independently wealthy and have no need for human interaction can be unconcerned about their reputation. For leaders in business and government, their reputation is their most valuable asset. Your reputation determines the quality and quantity of your interactions with others, especially people who can be of help. The people who give the least thought to their own reputations are the ones most likely to become parasites. Their reputation becomes their own worst enemy.

> *Probably the greatest harm done by vast wealth is the harm that we of moderate means do to ourselves when we let the vices of envy and hatred enter deep into our own natures.*
>
> Theodore Roosevelt (1858-1919)
> 26th U.S. President

If we evaluate our financial position in absolute terms, most of us would see that we are in pretty good shape. The great majority have adequate food, clothing, and shelter, plus many luxuries and conveniences that didn't even exist a generation ago. The average American today lives better than 99% of humans throughout history, including the average American of a generation or two ago.

We don't evaluate our financial position in absolute terms, though; we judge it in relative terms. We don't look to see if we have what we need; we look to see what others have. Our satisfaction is based on how we feel when we compare ourselves financially to others we observe.

Studies have shown that people have increased dissatisfaction when they lose financial position relative to others, even when their absolute financial position improves. For example, a man is in the 50th percentile in income; half make more; half make less. He gets a 10% raise and feels better about his financial position. Then he finds out that he is now in the 55th percentile in income. Despite his raise, the number of people making more than he does has increased from 50 to 55%. That one additional piece of information took that man from feeling better about his situation to feeling worse, even though he still has a 10% increase in income.

> *The darkest hour of any man's life is when he sits down to plan how to get money without earning it.*
>
> Horace Greeley (1811-1872)
> Newspaper Editor

We have progressed as a society to the point where it is extremely rare that someone must resort to crime to provide the necessities of life. We don't have to suffer the guilt of living in a society that creates characters like Oliver Twist or Jean Valjean. Today when people attempt to get money without earning it, they are motivated not by hunger, but usually by greed, sloth, or envy.

Nothing breeds envy and promotes criminal behavior like comparisons. Modern communications make comparisons not only easier, but inevitable. We can't avoid seeing what others earn and how they spend it; unfortunately, the ones who flaunt it seem to make the most for doing the least, which only increases the temptation to take shortcuts to wealth.

> *He that maketh haste to be rich shall not be innocent.*
>
> Proverbs 28:20

> *He who wishes to be rich in a day*
> *will be hanged in a year.*
>
> Leonardo da Vinci (1452-1519)
> Italian Artist, Inventor

Most of the imperfections we are saddled with don't rise to the level of vice. Most don't even meet the definition of habit. Most of our imperfections are simply part of our human nature, and they only reveal themselves in out-of-the-ordinary situations. Most of our behaviors do not merit any punishment, which is not to say that such behaviors do not have consequences. Sometimes the consequences of merely being human are more severe than the punishment of actually doing something bad.

In recent years a new field of study known as Behavioral Economics has emerged. Behavioral Economics developed as a legitimate field of study in large part because the way people should behave with money (according to traditional economists) is not the way they behave at all.

Traditional economists base their analyses and expectations of the economy on what people should logically do in given situations, which is the fatal flaw in their thinking. People rarely behave logically, especially when there is money involved.

> *Happy the man who has learned the cause of things*
> *and has put under his feet all fear, inexorable fate,*
> *and the noisy strife of the hell of greed.*
>
> Virgil (70-21 BC)
> Roman Poet

As a rule, human beings make decisions emotionally, then use whatever logic enables them to rationalize their decision. Even when we are aware we are making decisions in this manner, we are unlikely to admit to it. When it comes to irrational decisions about money, the two emotions that cause the most harm are greed and fear.

Greed is an emotion that has been most in evidence on Wall Street in recent years. The financial crisis that reached its nadir in 2008-2009 was triggered in large part by Wall Street firms taking huge risks with other peoples' money to maximize profits.

Then there is the greed of the individual stewards of others' assets. Such greed may be rather benign, as when a broker recommends an investment, not because it will benefit the client, but because the commission will benefit the broker.

There is the more malignant greed of the steward who overtly steals from clients to finance a certain lifestyle. I have read too many articles in recent years about corrupt financial advisors. They plundered the accounts of elderly clients to buy items like yachts, exotic cars, and Faberge' eggs.

> *Earth provides enough to satisfy every man's need, but not every man's greed.*
>
> Mohandas K. Gandhi (1869-1948)
> Indian Statesman

Even the little guy gets caught up in the emotion of greed. Something as simple as buying near the top of the market is a symptom of greed. That person is hoping that recent outstanding returns will continue indefinitely. Emotion overrules reason when people overpay for anything.

Using credit to purchase investments, whether stock, real estate, gold, whatever, is also a symptom of greed. The use of credit greatly increases the risks, but the desire for greater rewards, a symptom of greed in such cases, clouds one's judgment.

> *You try to be greedy when others are fearful and you try to be very fearful when others are greedy.*
>
> Warren Buffett (1930-)
> Investor, Philanthropist

The average person's approach to investing doesn't seem dysfunctional to that person, unless it is compared to buying and selling a different, more tangible item.

If you were in the market for a pair of shoes that has a typical price of $100, you would not likely buy them if the price rose to $200. On the other hand, if the price dropped to $50, you would probably buy as many pairs as you could afford to take advantage of the sale.

Do average people buy stocks that way? No - they tend to do just the opposite. When the market is in full bull mode and stock prices are well above their historic averages, people can't buy them fast enough. When we are in a severe bear market, and prices may be half of their historic average price, you can't give the darn things away.

> *In prosperity, caution; in adversity, patience.*
>
> Dutch Proverb

We have similar dysfunctions when it comes to holding on to investments in bad times. Because we can get daily, if not hourly, updates on our investment portfolios, we know exactly what someone else will pay for it at any given moment. If the amount they are willing to pay keeps going down, we panic and sell out of fear that the trend will continue and eventually our investments will be worthless.

Imagine if, every few days, you received an email telling you what others were willing to pay for your house on that day. Now suppose that for several weeks on end, the price that others were willing to pay kept dropping. Would you panic and sell out of fear that your house might soon become worthless? It's doubtful. You would likely become offended that these idiots keep annoying you with these emails on a subject about which they clearly know nothing. You would label them as spam and get on with your life.

> *By developing your discipline and courage, you can refuse to let other people's mood swings govern your financial destiny.*
>
> Ben Graham (1894-1976)
> Economist, Investor

If the previous scenario makes perfect sense when talking about your home, why do people not act the same way when it comes to their investments? Because your home is a very visible, tangible asset, it is easier to determine its value to you, even if that value differs from what others think. Your home has value as your home, not just as an investment in real estate. You may not like it if others denigrate your home by making low-ball offers, but it isn't likely to goad you into selling your house because you feel you know its worth better than they do.

When it comes to a basket of intangibles, like a stock portfolio, we are much less certain about what the true value is. We defer to the experts, in this case, "the market." If the market is down, it is because there are more sellers than buyers. If you join the ones who are panicking and selling, you are only contributing to the downslide.

> *The key to making money in stocks is not to get scared out of them.*
>
> Peter Lynch (1944-)
> Investor

If everyone knows that the key to making money with any investment is to buy low and sell high, why do people consistently do the opposite? The biggest reason why people tend to buy high and sell low is because that is what most of the other people are doing. When prices get too high, it's because more people are buying than selling, and when they get too low, it's because the majority is doing just the opposite.

Even though it is easier to march along with the

herd, it is the few who are willing to run counter to the herd who reap the profits. The average investor reaps about one-third of the actual gains of his/her investments, which is the result of buying high and selling low. Where does the other two-thirds go? It goes to the person on the other end of the trade who is willing to buy from others' fears and sell to their greed. Those people are being richly rewarded for being different.

> *The desire for safety stands against every great and noble enterprise.*
>
> Tacitus (56-117)
> Roman Senator

Mankind's ability to adapt to changes in our environment is one of the reasons we have become the dominant species on the planet. Adaptation is a good thing - mostly.

No one likes to be taken for granted, although there isn't a human being alive that doesn't take someone for granted occasionally. Taking someone or something for granted is a manifestation of adaptation. We adapt to those closest to us and come to expect that they will continue to do what they have always done for us. We adapt to our surroundings, especially if those surroundings are comfortable. If something or someone is to our liking, it takes no effort to get used to it.

> *Mankind, by the perverse depravity of their nature, esteem that which they have most desired as of no value the moment it is possessed, and torment themselves with fruitless wishes for that which is beyond their reach.*
>
> Francois Fenelon (1651-1715)
> French Archbishop

We adapt quickly to improvements in our material condition. A pay raise will be absorbed so quickly in increased spending we soon wonder how we ever got along with our old income. Our new, improved car, TV, smartphone, or job quickly becomes the new minimum acceptable standard, even when it was just a dream a few months before.

Adaptation causes us to shortchange ourselves on the pleasure of having something new and better. Since improvements in technology come at an ever-faster rate, we barely get used to a new gadget before an improved version is introduced.

Apple has been a great innovator with products like iPods, iPads, and iPhones. But even as their customers camp out to be the first to get the latest product, their enjoyment is already being tempered by the knowledge that Apple will soon introduce a newer, better version that will ruin their enjoyment of a product they don't even yet possess.

> *Is not dread of thirst when your well is full, the thirst that is unquenchable?*
>
> Kahlil Gibran (1883-1931)
> Poet, Philosopher

The younger and/or wealthier someone is, the more susceptible they are to the downsides of adaptation. You never see old people camping out to be the first one to get the new iPhone. When you grew up before the advent of television, not only do you not clamor for a phone that has internet, a camera, music, email, plus thousands of apps, such a device probably intimidates the hell out of you. The status quo is the friend of the old, but not the young.

Our unceasing desire to make things better and to make more of them is part of the human makeup, and America has turned that desire into an art form and has created the largest economy in history. And yet, how often do we take a break from our quest for something new to appreciate anew what we already have? When was the last time you went through a drawer, a trunk, or a closet, found some item that was once near and dear to your heart, and rediscovered the pleasure that it gave you all those years ago?

> *Every gain made by individuals or societies is almost instantly taken for granted. The luminous ceiling toward which we raise our longing eyes becomes, when we have climbed to the next floor, a stretch of disregarded linoleum beneath our feet.*
>
> Aldous Huxley (1894-1963)
> English Writer

The law of marginal utility states that the more we have of something, the less we value each additional unit. For example, if you have a million dollars, an extra ten dollars doesn't do much for you. On the other hand, if all you have is ten dollars, an extra ten makes a huge difference. Because even the poor in America have more possessions than most of the rest of the world, we don't fully appreciate all that we have.

> *He who gains a victory over other men is strong;*
> *but he who gains a victory over himself is all powerful.*
>
> Lao Tzu (5th Century BC)
> Chinese Philosopher
>
> *I count him braver who overcomes his desires than him who conquers his enemies;*
> *for the hardest victory is the victory over self.*
>
> Aristotle (384-322 BC)
> Greek Philosopher

Lao-Tzu and Aristotle never knew each other. No one in either part of those worlds even knew of the existence of that other part of the world. Yet both men, more than four hundred years before Christ, expressed the same thought in almost the exact same words.

Perhaps no part of ourselves is harder to control than our emotions. Victory over our emotions is victory over self.

We are not talking here about the ability to express emotions. One of the hallmarks of the present time is that people are encouraged to express their emotions. Expressing emotions is generally healthy, healthier than repressing them and letting the stress of repression lead to ulcers, migraines, and strokes.

There is a difference, however, between expressing emotions and surrendering to emotions. It is perfectly alright, even healthy, to express your fears about a declining stock market threatening your retirement portfolio. However, expressing those fears sometimes makes it easier to act on those fears. When that happens, expression of that emotion goes from being healthy to unhealthy to your physical and psychological well-being, as well as to your retirement portfolio.

> *The plans of the diligent lead surely to advantage,*
> *but everyone who is hasty comes surely to poverty.*
> Proverbs 21:5

Emotions prompt us to action, but acting on our emotions is almost always bad in the long run. When we act on our emotions, we are usually trying to accomplish one of two things - create pleasure or avoid pain. Either of these powerful drives can lead us to hasty actions that have adverse consequences.

Many people buy or lease cars they know they can't afford. They find themselves in such a situation because they ignored the previous quote. They were not diligent in determining just how much car they could afford. They did not do adequate research into finding out what cars would fall within their budget. Finally, they let their emotions get the best of them when they saw a new car in the showroom, smelled that new car smell, sat in those heated leather seats, cranked up the 300 watt stereo, and felt the surge of that powerful engine. The problem was that they were seduced by the upscale car that was out of their price range, and they were too hasty to close the deal.

> *A man who has committed a mistake and doesn't correct it is committing another mistake.*
> Confucius (551-479 BC)
> Chinese Philosopher

Once we find ourselves in such a situation, we are often reluctant to take steps to correct our mistake because before we can correct our mistake, we must admit our mistake. Admitting mistakes is not easy for anyone because the emotion of pride gets in the way.

Admitting a mistake to ourselves is bad enough, but admitting it to others, whether to parents, children, spouses, or others is a humbling experience. Often, the people to whom we have to admit a mistake have been harmed by our mistake and may have advised us against the action we took. All of which makes it that much harder to admit our mistake and take steps to undo the damage.

> *All problems become smaller if you don't dodge them but confront them. Touch a thistle timidly and it pricks you; grasp it boldly and its spines crumble.*
> William F. Halsey (1882-1959)
> Admiral, U.S. Navy

Because we are reluctant to first admit and then

correct our financial mistakes, they continue to prick us. The person who spends too much for a car gets pricked monthly for four, five, six, even seven years. Every car payment that is in excess of what should have been spent reduces funding for items that truly need funding, like retirement, home maintenance, or emergency savings. It may be a blow to one's pride to sell a car that should never have been bought in the first place, but that single blow to one's pride is preferable to the death by a thousand cuts to one's financial security by a never-ending stream of car payments.

> *The idea that God would take his attention away from the universe in order to give me a bicycle is just so unlikely I can't go along with it.*
>
> Quentin Crisp (1908-1999)
> English Raconteur

When we want something badly enough, we can delude ourselves in a variety of ways to justify obtaining the object of our desire.

One of the more amusing, and potentially dangerous, rationalizations I have heard involves invoking God. The rationalizations are along the lines of, "We prayed about it, and we know God wants us to have this (object of our desire)." If God wants you to have something, God will provide you with the means of acquiring it **first**. The creator of the universe does not put the cart before the horse. Only people make that kind of mistake.

The more we pay for something we desire,

whether in money, time, work, or a combination of sacrifices, the more we are likely to suffer the emotion of regret later. We are not very good at calculating future happiness. We are also not very good at judging past happiness, either.

> *One sees the past better than it was;*
> *one finds the present worse than it is;*
> *one hopes for a future happier than it will be.*
> Madame d'Epinay (1726-1783)
> French Writer

The emotion of nostalgia clouds our judgment of both the past and the present. The human memory does an incredible amount of filtering in order to retain a lifetime of information. In our recollection of the past, we tend to filter out negative aspects from the past. That's only natural because we can only remember so many details, we want our memories to be pleasant, and filtering out the "impurities" enables us to remember more things the way we want to remember them.

Remembering the past through the gauze of our memory can affect our actions in the present, as well as our appreciation of the present. A distorted view of the past leads to a distorted view of the present, which can only suffer in comparison to an idealized view of the past. If we can remember that the good old days were not really as good as we remember them, today begins to look a whole lot better.

> *An optimist sees an opportunity in every calamity; a pessimist sees a calamity in every opportunity.*
> Winston Churchill (1874-1965)
> British Prime Minister

Idealizing the past leads to underestimating the quality of the present, which leads one toward pessimism. There are good and bad aspects to every era. If I remember the '70's with any affection, it is because I remember it as the decade I graduated high school and college, moved to a new state, started a career, and met my wife. I don't dwell on our defeat in Vietnam, Watergate, oil embargoes, stagflation, or disco. If I did, I would remember that Doonesbury referred to the '70's as "a kidney stone of a decade."

If a distorted view of the past affects our appreciation of the present, it also cripples our ability to be optimistic about the future. If we think the past was better than it was and, as a result, we think the present is worse than it is, we will extrapolate that train of thought and assume that the future will be worse than the present, which we already hold in low esteem.

> *There is no security on this earth – only opportunity.*
> Douglas MacArthur (1880-1964)
> General, U.S. Army

When we become pessimistic, we focus on security instead of opportunity. We think of the future as something to survive instead of enjoy. We stop connecting with others through organizations like churches and Rotary Clubs. We buy gold and guns instead of stocks and bonds.

Pessimism is a self-fulfilling prophecy in that pessimists create a future in which no one wants to live. Only optimists are willing to do the work that is necessary to create a future that is better than the present. Only optimists are willing to take risks now that are necessary to earn rewards in the future.

> *Far better it is to dare mighty things, to win glorious triumphs, even though checkered by failure, than to take rank with those poor spirits who neither enjoy much nor suffer much, for they live in the gray twilight that knows not victory nor defeat.*
>
> Theodore Roosevelt (1858-1919)
> 26th U.S. President

Everything worth having has its price. I'm not referring to material possessions in this context. Material possessions have a price, but that price is in dollars, and it is easy to determine if that price is one you are willing to pay. I refer here to those intangibles that should not have a dollar value placed upon them.

A successful marriage requires giving up some individuality for the sake of the partnership. Being a good parent does not guarantee your children will turn out like you expect. Being a good son or daughter does not guarantee the approval of your parents. Friendship is not always reciprocated. Rewards will not always be commensurate with the risks taken and the effort given.

Those things most worth having do come at a price, but it is not a firm, fixed price for everyone. One couple may glide through a half-century of marriage with hardly a ripple, while another couple may be on the brink of divorce every other year. One person may barely crack a book while making the dean's list at college, while another studies constantly to keep off academic probation. One person's business may practically hemorrhage profits, while another wilts from a lack of customers.

> *What is a cynic? A man who knows the price of everything and the value of nothing.*
>
> Oscar Wilde (1854-1900)
> Irish Writer, Poet

Those things most worth having are only available to those who are willing to pay the price, while having no certainty of what that price will ultimately be. Only an optimist is willing to pay an uncertain price for something of inestimable value.

We live in an era of unbridled emotions, and we have paid a price for it. We get too high, then we get too low, and our finances get whipsawed in the process. We could use some of the stoicism of the ancient Spartans or the stiff-upper-lip attitude of the British during the Blitzkrieg.

Our unbridled emotions do more to hurt us financially, individually, and nationally than any other single factor. The good news is our emotions are the one factor affecting our finances that we have the ability to control. As long as our emotions continue to control us, we will have good reason to be pessimistic.

> *Hell is the state in which we are barred from receiving what we truly need because of the value we give to what we merely want.*
>
> Virgil (70-21 BC)
> Roman Poet
>
> *Americans define a need as a 48-hour old want.*
>
> George Will (1941-)
> Journalist, Author

We put ourselves through Hell getting things we think we need, only to find out after a while that not only didn't we need them, we didn't really want them much, either. Such mistakes wouldn't be a major problem except that in satisfying our short-term wants, we sacrifice our ability to satisfy our long-term needs.

When someone "needs" a new car and buys or leases twice as much car as is needed and, at the same time, is not adequately funding his/her retirement account, that person is putting short-term wants above long-term needs. When someone "needs" a vacation, but the money spent on a vacation means that person no longer has the money to pay for an adequate life insurance policy to protect his/her children, that person is putting short-term wants above long-term needs.

Need is not measured by someone's level of desire for something. Need is measured by the negative effects on a person that are beyond that person's control if what is needed is withheld. We need, air, food, water, and sleep. If we do not receive a sufficient amount of all of these requirements, we will die.

As a species, we need sex to continue the species. As individuals, we don't need sex to survive. Nature has designed sex to be something we want badly enough that we think of it as something we need, thus insuring the survival of the species. Sex is merely the strongest and most prevalent example of how strong desires can cause us to confuse wants with needs.

Semper inops quicumque cupit.
(Whoever desires is always poor.)

Claudius (10 BC-54 AD)
Roman Emperor

The inability to control one's desires leads inevitably to an inability to control one's spending. Most of our desires can be satisfied through some financial transaction, which can lead to financial problems in the present and the future. The inability to control one's desires is also a habit that gets worse over time, guaranteeing that one's financial problems will also get worse over time.

Ill-luck is almost always the result of taking pleasure first and duty second, instead of duty first and pleasure second.

Theodore T. Munger (1830-1910)
Clergyman

It is our duty to take care of our needs and the needs of those who depend on us. It is our pleasure to take care of our wants and the wants of those we love. Duty involves making a sacrifice now for something better in the future. Pleasure involves living for the moment, with no thought to the future.

> *The true way to gain much is never desire to gain too much. He is not rich that possesses much, but he that covets no more; and he is not poor that enjoys little, but he that wants too much.*
>
> Francis Beaumont (1584-1616)
> English Dramatist
>
> *Misfortunes always come in by the door that has been left open for them.*
>
> Czech Proverb

When we are constantly in pursuit, we are not in a position to receive. Good things come to those who wait, but good things also come to those who aren't running around chasing after whatever has just lit the spark of desire. We associate action with progress, but, very often, the best way to attract what you want is to be still and at peace and let the object of your desire come to you.

> *One great difference between a wise man and a fool is the former only wishes for what he may possibly obtain; the latter desires impossibilities.*
>
> Democritus (460-370 BC)
> Greek Philosopher

> *All the money in the world is no use to a man or his country if he spends it as fast as he makes it. All he has left is his bills and the reputation for being a fool.*
>
> Rudyard Kipling (1865-1935)
> English Poet, Novelist

The wisest man is the one who controls his desires, rather than letting his desires control him. Such men (and women) are scarce, and they not only control their lives, but come in time to control others' lives as well. Next in line is the man who has desires within his ability to attain, which can be a mixed blessing, as obtaining one's desires provides positive reinforcement to a behavior that may be harmful in the long run. Finally, there's the fool who chases after impossibilities. The fool sees zero return for his investment of time, effort, and money.

You can tell the difference between these three types with the following example. The first man doesn't play the lottery because he knows the odds are ridiculously long, and both his time and his money are too valuable to waste on it. The second man invests in his retirement plan, but buys a lottery ticket every week because "you never know." The last man buys a hundred lottery tickets a week because that is his retirement plan.

We have been descending into a culture of victimization for at least two decades now. People are quite willing to accept risks when they consider the upside, but when a negative outcome occurs, those same people are looking for someone other than themselves to take the blame (and pay for their financial loss, as well as their pain and suffering).

Consider smokers in the U.S. Since 1965, cigarette makers have been required to print warnings on every pack of cigarettes. The date of this requirement means that anyone one who started smoking after 1965 (which means almost everyone born after 1950) knew the risks the first time they lit up. Still, you hear of lawsuits and multi-million dollar awards being given to people who chose to smoke, despite being warned of the dangers before they ever started, with the warnings coming directly from the manufacturer of the product.

It is impossible to protect people from themselves if they don't first accept the responsibility to protect themselves. Pleasure-seeking often involves risky behavior. One way to reduce risky behavior is to reduce submission to desires. Unfortunately, the same people who are the weakest when it comes to controlling themselves are also the first ones to look for someone else to blame when the chickens come home to roost.

For even when we were with you, we used to give you this order: if anyone is not willing to work, then he is not to eat, either. For we hear that some among you are leading an undisciplined life, doing no work at all.

2 Thessalonians 3:10-11

Poverty is not dishonorable in itself, but only when it comes from idleness, intemperance, extravagance, and folly.

Plutarch (46-120)
Greek Historian

You can divide a population into four different types of people. The first, and best, are those rare few who are looking for nothing-for-something. These are the people who only think of giving, never taking. Anonymous philanthropists and saints fall into this category.

Next we have those who are looking for something-for-something. This is the group that includes most of us. These people believe in paying their own way, in free and fair markets, and in the principle that first you give, and then you receive.

Third is a group as rare as the first one. These are the people who are looking for nothing-for-nothing. They are rare because, in order to be looking for nothing, you have to be totally self-sufficient and independent. Our lives have become too complex and intertwined to enable someone to live in such isolation. We have also become so specialized in our skill sets that trade with other people is more necessary than ever in order to survive. This group may not take anything from the rest of humanity, but they don't add anything, either.

Finally, we have the bottom of the barrel - those who are looking for something-for-nothing, or at least something-for-less-than-something. It's not easy being a something-for-nothing person. If you give nothing for something, you don't get repeat business, which requires you to constantly find new hosts to continue your parasitic ways. Something-for-nothings make up for their relatively small numbers by creating big disasters wherever they go.

> *There is hardly anything in the world that some man can't make a little worse and sell a little cheaper, and the people who consider price only are this man's lawful prey.*
>
> John Ruskin (1819-1900)
> English Art Critic
>
> *Did you get your money by fraud? By pandering to men's vices or men's stupidity? By catering to fools, in the hope of getting more than your ability deserves? By lowering your standards? By doing work you despise for purchasers you scorn? If so, then your money will not give you a moment's or a penny's worth of joy. Then all the things you buy will become, not a tribute to you, but a reproach; not an achievement, but a reminder of shame.*
>
> Ayn Rand (1905-1982)
> Novelist, Philosopher

The person whose aim is to give less than what is equitable or to take more than is earned is the one who is potentially the most damaging to society. Such people are dangerous for two reasons. First, they can be hard to detect and they can take advantage of others for years, even decades, before their reputation finally destroys them. Second, and perhaps more important, this person dwells inside all of us, at least from time to time.

Even the most upright, honest, hardworking person has taken advantage of the occasional opportunity to cut a corner, thumb the scale, or shirk a duty at work. It's impossible to work thirty or forty years and never give in to such opportunities. The danger from the person who behaves this way all the time is serious. Even more serious is the danger posed when good people in the something-for-something group give in to the lure of something-for-less-than-something. That kind of decay from within can be hard to stop once it takes hold.

> *Doing for people what they can and ought to do for themselves is a dangerous experiment. In the last analysis, the welfare of the workers depends upon their own initiative. Whatever is done under the guise of philanthropy or social morality which in any way lessens initiative is the greatest crime that can be committed against the toilers.*
>
> Samuel Gompers (1850-1924)
> Labor Union Leader

Just as it is in our nature to try to get more than we give in a transaction, it is also in our nature to try to avoid unpleasant tasks. For many people, one of life's unpleasant tasks is earning a living. It would be nice if everyone could love their job and could look forward to going out and earning a living every day. However, there will always be low-paying, unpleasant jobs that will need to be done. There will always be people who never find the right career, who spend their lives as a square peg in a round hole. There will always be people who prefer not to work, no matter the job. And so, there will always be people whose only reason for doing a job is the paycheck.

Initiative is one of the greatest human attributes,

and anything that stifles a person's initiative is detrimental to the individual and to society as a whole. Nothing stifles initiative like removing the necessity of performing a task. People don't have to rely on their initiative to do the things they want to do; they rely on their initiative to do the things they need to do.

When the necessity of doing something, such as earning an income or caring for one's children, is transferred from the individual to others or to the state, that individual's initiative is depleted.

Initiative is not something we compartmentalize. If our initiative to perform one duty is depleted, our initiative to perform our other duties is depleted, too. Well-intended but misguided efforts to do the duties of others have a corrosive effect on the intended beneficiary. Like corrosion, the effects are slow and subtle, but the damage is incessant and, if not stopped early on, will render the person useless.

> *A gift much expected is paid, not given.*
>
> George Herbert (1593-1633)
> English Poet, Priest
>
> *A proud man is seldom a grateful man,*
> *for he never thinks he gets as much as he deserves.*
>
> Henry Ward Beecher (1813-1887)
> Clergyman, Abolitionist
>
> *My pride fell with my fortunes.*
>
> William Shakespeare (1564-1616)
> English Playwright

If you've done much charity work in your life, at

some point you have probably been surprised at an apparent lack of gratitude by some recipients of that charity. If it happens often enough, it can diminish your desire to be charitable in the future.

Some of the apparent lack of gratitude by some can be explained by our ever-increasing entitlement mentality. If someone is entitled to something, there should be no need to express gratitude to anyone. Viewing charity as an entitlement removes the stigma of being someone who has to rely on charity. One problem with such a perception is if the charity ceases, the recipient becomes angry, not that charity ceased, but that an entitlement has been stolen.

You can think about such behavior in another context. You would expect that the French and the Iraqi peoples would both be grateful to America - after all, we liberated both of them from the yoke of oppression. We're not particularly loved in either country, though the reason isn't ingratitude, it's pride. In both countries, Americans did what, from the perspective of the French and the Iraqis, should have been done by themselves. To be saved from one's helplessness is a reminder of that helplessness, and the more helpless one feels, the less initiative one demonstrates in the future.

> *Don't expect to be paid a dollar an hour for your working hours when you then use your leisure hours as though they were not worth five cents a dozen.*
>
> Henry L. Doherty (1870-1939)
> Financier, Oilman

With the flood of new technology in the last couple of decades, the line between work and leisure is more blurred than ever. In many jobs, people can work from anywhere at any time. Leisure has invaded the workplace, but mostly in superficial ways like casual dress. Work has invaded leisure much more, simply because you're always connected to your work if you have nothing more than a smartphone.

Social media has also given everyone the chance to put their leisure activities out there for all the world, including current and potential employers, to see. Everyone has the right to use their leisure time as they wish, though leisure time is a valuable resource and shouldn't be squandered, either by debauchery or by more work. Knowing that your leisure life may now be scrutinized as closely as your work life by an employer, workers need to be sure that their leisure activities are not going to create a problem at work, and workers need to be ever more discreet about what leisure activities they make available through social media.

> *The common idea that success spoils people by making them vain, egotistic and self-complacent is erroneous; on the contrary, it makes them for the most part, humble, tolerant and kind. Failure makes people cruel and bitter.*
>
> W. Somerset Maugham (1874-1965)
> English Playwright, Novelist

> *There must be a reason why some people can afford to live well. They must have worked for it. I only feel angry when I see waste; when I see people throwing away things we could use.*
>
> Mother Teresa (1910-1997)
> Catholic Missionary

An abundance of money is unlikely to change one's character unless the money was not earned by the person who has it. If a man accumulates a million dollars over a decade of hard work and delayed gratification, that man will have the same character at the end of the decade that he had at the beginning. If another man wins a million dollars in the lottery, that person's character is more likely to be affected by the windfall, especially if he were not wealthy before. By the end of another decade, the man who earned a million dollars will likely have accumulated two or three million more. The man who won the lottery is likely to be broke, the money lost to frivolous spending, scams, and parasitic friends and relatives.

> *Ever wonder about those people who spend $2 apiece on those little bottles of Evian water? Try spelling Evian backward.*
>
> George Carlin (1937-2008)
> Comedian

In order to have a proper understanding of money when it comes to disbursing it, people first need a proper understanding of money when it comes to creating it. The harder and longer someone works to become wealthy, the less naïve they are likely to be when it comes to spending money. When money is given to someone and they didn't have to work for it, a lot of that money is likely to be spent wastefully. Even if someone earns money, but they earn a disproportionately large amount (athletes, movie stars, and CEOs, for example), a lot of that money may be spent frivolously, too. The more you put into getting your money, the more you expect to get **from** your money.

EXTERNAL EXCITATIONS

Even as you try to gain control over your behavior, others seem intent on undoing all your efforts.

Are you part of a typical American household? Probably not, since there is no typical American household, which could be defined as one where the major characteristics of that household are shared by a majority of the population. While there is no typical American household, allow me to create a hypothetical one for our purpose here.

Our American household in 2011 has two adults and two children. One adult works full-time, the other part-time. Their combined annual income is $65,000. They own a house valued at $150,000. They also owe $120,000 on their mortgage, $12,000 on one of their two cars, and a $2,000 average balance on their credit cards. Their total debt to income ratio is a fairly consistent 2:1.

Or is it? We have not factored in their share of the federal debt, which comes to $46,000 per person, or $184,000 for their four-person household (Kids have an equal piece of the debt in this hypothetical.) In addition to this current debt load, the federal government is currently adding $1.5 trillion to the total every year, which means that our hypothetical household's total share of the federal debt is increasing by $1,600 **per month.**

> *The budget should be balanced, the Treasury should be refilled, public debt should be reduced, the arrogance of officialdom should be tempered and controlled, and the assistance to foreign lands should be curtailed, lest Rome become bankrupt.*
>
> Cicero (106-43 BC)
> Roman Statesman

I need to provide a couple of definitions at this point. The federal **debt** is the total of all the money the federal government owes at a given moment. The federal **deficit** is the difference between federal revenues and expenditures for the current year. Every year, the deficit for that year is added to the federal debt. Deficit spending causes debt.

When media pundits and policy wonks begin discussing the federal debt and deficit, it's easy for most of us to disconnect. It's hard to get your mind around a figure like $15 trillion when a ten-dollar increase in the cable bill gives you a headache. If they would break these numbers down into what the average family's share is, a lot more people would appreciate the magnitude of the problem.

I believe a lot more people would also be driven to action if they fully understood their personal stake in government spending. Our hypothetical household works hard to pay their bills every month and to make a dent in their outstanding debt. If, after all their efforts, they still find themselves $1,600 deeper in debt every month because of someone else's spending, that is cause for action.

There are 10^{11} stars in the galaxy. That used to be a huge number. But it's only a hundred billion. It's less than the national deficit! We used to call them astronomical numbers. Now we should call them economical numbers.

Richard Feynman (1918-1988)
Physicist

A billion dollars here, a billion dollars there, and pretty soon you're talking about real money.

Everett Dirksen (1896-1969)
Member, U.S. Senate

The federal debt is roughly equal to all the outstanding mortgage debt in the U.S. To put it one way, if there were no federal debt, everyone who owns a home could own another one of similar value without increasing their debt load. To put it yet another way, the federal government has saddled every homeowner in the U.S. with a debt equal to their outstanding mortgage without giving them a second home to enjoy.

The American Republic will endure until the day Congress discovers that it can bribe the public with the public's money.

Alexis de Tocqueville (1805-1859)
French Historian

Why is our government in such dire financial straits? There are many reasons, but we need to boil it down to the most basic reasons that no one can refute. First, the population as a whole has demanded more from their government than they are willing to pay. Second, our elected officials will not say no to these demands if it means they will no longer be our elected officials.

Obviously, not everyone in our country is receiving a dollar's worth from the federal government while only paying in fifty-eight cents. In fact, hardly a soul would land right on the average input/outgo ratio for the government as a whole. Many pay a great deal and receive little, while many receive a great deal and pay nothing.

> *In general, the art of government consists in taking as much money as possible from one party of the citizens to give to the other.*
>
> Voltaire (1694-1778)
> French Writer, Philosopher
>
> *Any society that takes away from those most capable and gives to the least will perish.*
>
> Abraham Lincoln (1809-1965)
> 16th U.S. President
>
> *A government which robs Peter to pay Paul can always count on Paul's support.*
>
> George Bernard Shaw (1856-1950)
> Irish Playwright

Every popularly elected government struggles to find a proper balance between helping the poorest without decimating the richest. In a country as large and diverse as the U.S., there will always be people who need help from their government, just as there will always be people who are able and willing to provide that help. A properly run government will try to help the poor, but not so much that it stifles personal initiative. They will also ask the rich to fund that help, but not so much that it stifles the incentive to create wealth.

> *Taxes are paid in the sweat of every man who labors. If those taxes are excessive, they are reflected in idle factories, tax-sold farms and in hordes of hungry people, tramping the streets and seeking jobs in vain.*
>
> Franklin D. Roosevelt (1882-1945)
> 32nd U.S. President

The methods in which a government collects and distributes money are akin to the way the human organism keeps itself healthy. If the organism takes in too much food and doesn't use it, it goes to waste and makes the organism unhealthy. If it takes in too little food, the organism becomes weak in a variety of ways, since it cannot support its essential functions.

For the organism to grow healthily, the growth must be equitably distributed. Organs develop simultaneously with muscles, bones, and nerves. Delaying development in one area in order to speed up development of another area leads to a weakening of the entire organism.

When injury or disease harms part of the organism, resources are focused on healing the parts of the organism most injured or most essential to the life of the organism. When the crisis passes, the organism returns to its normal pattern of collection and distribution of nutrients.

> *Every new tax is immediately felt more or less by the people. It occasions always some murmur, and meets with some opposition... Debt is not immediately felt by the people, and occasions neither murmur nor complaint.*
>
> Adam Smith (1723-1790)
> Scottish Philosopher, Economist

The big difference between an organism and a government is that an organism must live in the present only. If an organism is hungry, it cannot borrow food from tomorrow in order to eat today. If it is suffocating at the moment, it cannot breathe next week's air. An organism must take care of itself every single day, because it cannot count on anything but the resources it can acquire today to keep it alive.

Governments, on the other hand, can borrow from the future to finance whatever they want to do today. This ability to tap into future resources can be essential to survival, as when our government borrowed billions to finance victory in World War II.

The ability to easily borrow from the future can also create great temptations. When you are a politician elected by the people, you can garner votes by promising to give them what they want without asking them to pay for it - now. Eventually, inevitably, such methods create problems, chaos, even disaster if unattended. When our hypothetical family's share of the federal debt is $184,000 and climbing $1,600 a month, we have definitely reached disaster stage if it continues unattended.

> *No government can guarantee security. It can only tax, production, distribution and service and gradually crush the power to pay taxes. That settles nothing. It only uses up the gains of the past and postpones the developments of the future.*
>
> Henry Ford (1863-1947)
> Founder, Ford Motor Company

Taxes are money that has been earned in the past. Debt is money that is expected (but not guaranteed) to be earned in the future. Which do you spend more carefully - money that has already been earned by labor you've already done or money that you will earn by labor you will do in the future? Studies show that people pay, on average, 19% more when they buy on credit than when they buy the same item for cash. If we discount the value of our own future labor by such an amount, imagine how much we discount the future labor of someone else. And we have been assuming for decades that the debt our government has been accumulating will be paid by "someone else." We expect that when the day of reckoning comes, we will either be dead or retired with our guaranteed social security and the power of our senior voting bloc.

> *Inflation is taxation without legislation.*
>
> Milton Friedman (1912-2006)
> Economist

You have to go back to the late '70's and early '80's to find a period of serious inflation in the U.S.

Even during that period, annual inflation was never more than 15%, which is uncomfortably high, but not catastrophic.

Between the end of World War I in 1918 and 1923, the value of the German paper Mark to the German gold Mark went from 1:1 to 1 trillion:1, meaning the German paper Mark was worthless. Germany had chosen to finance the war through debt rather than taxes, and the additional debt they incurred from the payment of war reparations paved the way for the rise of Adolf Hitler in the coming decade.

In recent years, Zimbabwe has had official annual inflation rates as high as 11 million percent. This hyperinflation was caused by the government printing money as needed, with nothing to back it up. Printing more money does not create wealth, it only devalues the currency. Zimbabwe's attempt to create wealth where none existed only served to destroy what wealth had existed in the form of their currency.

In order to increase the money supply and stimulate the economy, the federal government has implemented a program called quantitative easing. A central bank initiates quantitative easing by purchasing financial assets with money that it creates electronically. They don't even bother to print the paper money; they create it with a few keystrokes. In a slow economy, the risks of inflation caused by quantitative easing are small. However, if quantitative easing has the desired results, that additional money created from thin air will create a higher rate of inflation in the future.

There is far more danger in a public monopoly than there is in a private monopoly, for when the government goes into business it can always shift its losses to the taxpayer. The government never really goes into business, for it never makes ends meet, and that is the first requisite of business. It just mixes a little business with a lot of politics, and no one ever gets a chance to find out what is actually going on.

Thomas A. Edison (1847-1931)
Inventor, Businessman

When everybody has got money they cut taxes,
and when they're broke they raise taxes.
That's statesmanship of the highest order.

Will Rogers (1879-1935)
Humorist, Actor

We've all seen pie charts used for financial illustration purposes. Let's take it a step further and think of an actual pizza pie. When the economy is doing well, the pizza is large, and the government doesn't need a big slice of a large pizza. When the economy is doing poorly, the government needs a bigger slice of that smaller pizza in order to get the same amount of pizza they had before. They could just take less pizza, but entitlements force them to take a minimum amount of pizza, even if that means that others receive far less. Of course, they can also borrow someone else's pizza, which they have been doing more and more in recent years. When it's time to pay that pizza back, we will be going hungry for quite a long time to come.

Creative Destruction was a term coined by

Joseph Schumpeter in his 1942 book, *Capitalism, Socialism, and Democracy*. Creative destruction occurs when something newer and better comes along and kills its predecessor. Free markets let creative destruction occur because it is best for everyone in the long run. Digital picture-taking almost killed Kodak, but limitless high-quality photography is now available to everyone who can afford a digital camera or cell phone.

No one but a government official would consider impeding that kind of progress in order to keep a few thousand employed in an antiquated industry. Creative destruction isn't always pretty, especially if it's your job and your employer that are being destroyed, but the process is as necessary to a healthy economy as the replacement of old cells with new ones is to an organism.

Those who look to government to generate prosperity believe that, in our economic engine, private enterprises are the moving parts and government is the gasoline. In truth, private enterprise is the gasoline, and the workers and the customers are the moving parts. What is government's role? Government is the oil in the economic engine. Oil is not fuel; it is a lubricant. Oil does not power the engine, but without oil the engine will seize up and be rendered useless. Oil has a vital role to play in an engine's performance, but oil is confined to certain parts of the engine, and is not allowed to mix with gasoline. When they invade each other's space, both oil and gasoline's ability to do their jobs are compromised.

> *A multitude of laws in a country is like a great number of physicians, a sign of weakness and malady.*
>
> Voltaire (1694-1778)
> French Writer, Philosopher
>
> *If you have ten thousand regulations you destroy all respect for the law.*
>
> Winston Churchill (1874-1965)
> British Prime Minister

Why do we have fifty different titles in the Code of Federal Regulations (with thousands of regulations under each title), but we only have Ten Commandments?

Government intrusion most often takes the form of burdensome regulations. These regulations may have a noble purpose, but often their effect is to suffocate the economic engine. There is the time and expense of trying to meet several, and often conflicting, regulations. The difficulty in meeting these regulations often leads to a disregard of the regulations, either by intent or ignorance.

God limited his Commandments to ten for a reason. He knows we aren't very bright, and ten is about our limit when it comes to remembering something. (Can you recite all Ten Commandments right now?) Also, when there are only ten rules to follow, no one can claim ignorance of the law. The greater the number of rules and regulations, the greater the percentage of rules and regulations that will be overlooked, ignored, or intentionally disobeyed. A profusion of little rules makes it that much harder to enforce the big rules.

> *I firmly believe that the army of persons who urge greater and greater centralization of authority and greater and greater dependence upon the Federal Treasury are really more dangerous to our form of government than any external threat that can possibly be arrayed against us.*
>
> Dwight D. Eisenhower (1890-1969)
> 34th U.S. President

Like Ancient Rome at its peak, the U.S. today has little to fear from outside attackers. That is not to say we are immune from attack. Like Ancient Rome, we can defeat anyone who might attack us, which discourages attack from without.

Our danger lies, not in attack from without, but in decay from within. The Roman Empire became more decadent over the centuries, which enabled its enemies to take advantage of weaknesses the Romans did not previously have. The more dependent the individual becomes on the government, the more the government and the individual are weakened. These weaknesses will then be exploited. There will be real enemies who will try to exploit our weaknesses to destroy us. There will also be those who are not our enemies, but merely our competitors. They will exploit our weaknesses to defeat us, not in military conflict, but in economic competition.

There is nothing like competition to sharpen one's game, and we have not had stiff competition in the marketplace for quite some time. We have certainly lost thousands of jobs to foreign competition, but we have also created new jobs and more skilled jobs to replace them. We have been secure in our position as the world's leading economic power. However, as our debt rises, our capital investment shrinks, and our productivity lags, our competitors can sense the tide turning.

> *If ever this free people, if this government itself is ever utterly demoralized, it will come from this incessant human wriggle and struggle for office, which is but a way to live without work.*
>
> Abraham Lincoln (1809-1965)
> 16th U.S. President

If we are going to demand that government spend less, we will also have to expect less from government. When nearly half the money the government spends is borrowed, it is safe to say that hardly a soul in the country is receiving less than he or she is paying. That hypothetical family we looked at earlier is no exception. They pay taxes, but they are likely receiving government benefits, either directly or indirectly, that exceed the value of their payments.

For example, if defense spending this year is $550 billion, and the U.S. population is 310 million, the per capita bill to finance defense spending is $1,775 per person, or $7,100 for a family of four. Our hypothetical family likely paid less than that in income taxes, so they did not even cover their portion of being protected from attack. Someone had to pay the difference on that, not to mention the cost of all the other benefits the family received, from education for the kids to roads to take them to work and school.

When we begin to realize that all of us are getting more than we are currently paying, we are prompted to do two things. First, we demand greater care in the spending of our tax dollars. We will take on the responsibility to ask questions such as, do we really need to spend $1,775 per person per year to be safe? Second, we will recognize and accept that, even as we demand that the government spend less and provide more value for what they spend, it will also be necessary for everyone to pay more if these deficits are going to be reduced enough to make a difference.

Our federal debt now equals our annual national GDP, which means that it would take every dollar earned by every man, woman, and child over the next year to pay off what we owe. That could only be done if we all went on a year-long fast, didn't pay any of our bills, and simply turned over every cent to the U.S. Treasury. Since we can't do anything remotely close to that, it will be a long time getting our debt down to a manageable level, even with painful steps taken.

When we live our personal lives with ever-increasing debt, we are at least aware that such a pattern cannot go on forever. We can remain in denial for only so long because every month the bills come in and we are reminded of just how deep a hole we have dug for ourselves. We know on some level that it must all end, and end badly, unless we take serious action to reverse the trend. We may contemplate bankruptcy, which is often only a temporary fix, as the real problem is a habit of spending more than we earn, and until that cycle is broken, financial peace will never come.

Government debt is more destructive for several reasons. First, bankruptcy is not an option. It might be tempting to think that the U.S. could just walk away from several trillions of dollars in debt obligations, but if that ever happened, the collapse of the world economy would make the Depression '30's look like the Roaring '20's.

Second, government debt is an orphan - no one wants to accept that they have contributed to the problem. Even those who pay in nothing and receive much feel no responsibility because what they receive is labeled "entitlements." Such labeling removes the stigma of charity, but also makes it far more difficult to reduce what is being given.

> *No single raindrop believes it is to blame for the flood.*
>
> Popular Poster
> Despair.com

Finally, government debt is worse than personal debt because we can delude ourselves longer about the day of reckoning. Imagine how you would feel if, every month, along with your regular bills, you also received a statement from the U.S. Treasury, stating your household's liability for the federal debt. For our hypothetical household, that liability is currently about $184,000 and goes up about $1,600 per month. There might be no minimum payment due, but the huge balance due and the never-ending accumulation of principal and interest would be enough to make most people sick, then galvanize them to take action. The one thing that a monthly statement wouldn't do is allow anyone the continued luxury of remaining ignorant on just how serious the nation's and, by extension, their personal situations really are.

> *They that will not be counseled cannot be helped. If you do not hear reason she will rap you on the knuckles.*
>
> Benjamin Franklin (1706-1790)
> Founding Father
>
> *We ask advice, but we seek approbation.*
>
> Charles Caleb Colton (1780-1832)
> English Cleric, Writer

I have not yet determined whether the increasing political polarization in the U.S. is a symptom or a cause of something larger. There is no doubt that we have become more polarized in our politics over the last couple of decades.

The media have either caused or at least capitalized on this polarization, depending on your point of view. In either case, there is no shortage of media outlets that cater to either a liberal or a conservative viewpoint.

The trend in providing news that caters to a particular point of view is the result of the tendency people have for **Confirmation Bias**. Confirmation Bias is a tendency to search for or interpret information in a way that confirms one's preconceptions. If we hold a particular point of view, we seek out, consciously or unconsciously, sources that confirm that we are correct in our thinking. We want to think we are seeking illumination when, in fact, we are seeking only validation.

Because validation is easier to obtain than illumination, people rarely become wiser; they merely become more entrenched in their ways of thinking and acting. Such behavior occurs in our financial, as well as our political, lives. Books on how to make a killing in various markets greatly outsell books on how to become thriftier because our bias has always been toward getting more, not needing less. Books that don't confirm what you already believe are a tough sell, which is why those books on how to make a killing with some investment aren't going to tell you that any investment that enables you to make a killing is equally capable of killing you.

> *Most men believe that it would benefit them if they could get a little from those who have more. How much more it would benefit them if they would learn a little from those who know more.*
>
> William Boetcker (1873-1962)
> Presbyterian Minister

People are no different when it comes to seeking financial advice from a person. There are approximately 63,000 Certified Financial Planners in the U.S., which is one for every five-thousand

Americans. CFPs should be completely overwhelmed by the sheer number of people seeking their advice. As a CFP, I can tell you that is not the case.

Certified Financial Planners have an ethical obligation to tell their clients what they need to hear, which is very often not what they want to hear. As a result, people will gravitate to a "financial advisor" who will tell them that they don't need to spend less and save more; they merely need to buy this particular financial product that will solve all their financial problems. The difference between the two is like the difference between a doctor who tells you to lose weight by eating healthier and exercising more and a salesman who says you can lose that weight by just taking this little pill he's selling. We know to whom people prefer to listen, and we know who has a solution that might actually work.

One reason people look for a miracle financial cure is that we have been sold an idealized view of retirement, usually by firms that are trying to sell us something. Most of us have seen marketing material for a financial product aimed at those at or near retirement. There are pictures of a grey-haired (but still attractive) couple golfing, sailing, walking on the beach, etc. The implication is here you see what successful people do in retirement, and you can do these things too, if you only purchase their product.

Such a retirement has appeal if you loathe your current job, which probably feels more like serving time than merely marking time. The contrast between where you are and where the people in the brochure are is so stark that you will naturally want what they have and will pay for it. That idealized view of retirement also has the effect of increasing anyone's unhappiness on the job, simply by making such a comparison.

If you think about retirement a week at a time, you can see through the imagery. There are three periods a day (morning, afternoon, and evening) and seven days a week. That's twenty-one squares a week that have to be filled with something. Even if you fill five of them with golf, you still have sixteen left. Most of the activities with which we expect to fill those squares cost money, too. The people who can afford to live such a retirement are likely to be so successful they don't want to retire from what they do, and they are in the position they can do those things on a regular basis without having to retire.

> *Advice after injury is like medicine after death.*
>
> Danish Proverb
>
> *Advice is what we ask for when we already know the answer but wish we didn't.*
>
> Erica Jong (1942-)
> Author

Receiving unsolicited advice after something bad has occurred can be annoying. Soliciting advice after you've done something bad can be frustrating to whomever you're soliciting. The best advice is that which is solicited before you take any action and that you are willing to follow because you trust the advisor to give you advice which will lead to the outcome that is best for you in the long run.

There is nothing more frustrating in my profession than to be contacted by someone who is now seeking advice on how to extricate themselves from a situation they wouldn't be in if they had solicited advice before they took an action. The main reason they didn't solicit advice beforehand is they knew they would be advised against doing whatever it is they were determined to do. When the unpleasant yet totally foreseeable result happens, the advisor can usually help only to the extent that he or she can turn back the hands of time.

The wise man sees in the misfortune of others what he should avoid.

Publilius Syrus (1st Century BC)
Latin Writer

There's no education in the second kick of a mule.

Ernest F. Hollings (1922-)
Member, U.S. Senate

At the very least, we should learn from our mistakes. At the very best, we should learn from the mistakes of others and avoid altogether the behavior that creates problems. At the very worst, we keep making the same mistakes, somehow thinking that this time it will be different. Those who fall into the first category comprise the majority of us. Those who fall in the second category are the most successful among us. Those who fall in the last category literally fall to the bottom. The only thing that keeps the last group from making the same mistake in perpetuity is the evaporation of funding.

> *Few people at the beginning of the nineteenth century needed an adman to tell them what they wanted.*
>
> J. K. Galbraith (1908-2006)
> Economist

Advertising is basically the creation of desire where it didn't previously exist. Advertising became effective in the twentieth century because of several factors. The Industrial Revolution created a large class of people with disposable income. New forms of communication enabled more people to be reached by advertising. Finally, more people were concentrated in cities, which made advertising more effective and which reduced distribution costs.

Studies have shown that the average American eight-year-old has a vocabulary of four-thousand words, of which four-hundred are brand names. While estimates vary widely, the most reliable data suggests that the average American is subjected to about three-thousand marketing messages a day. These messages would include overt advertising like billboards and TV commercials, but also include more subtle messages like seeing a logo on clothes, cars, or computers. With that much constant pounding, you tune out most of what we see and hear, but you don't get hit three-thousand times a day without some of those punches getting through.

As part of the goal of creating desire for a product, advertising attempts to make you feel dissatisfied with your present situation. Most people are very happy with their state-of-the-art gadget right up to the moment that it is no longer state-of-the-art. The functionality of their gadget has not changed, only the reference point has. The way to get people to spend money they normally wouldn't spend is to make them feel that they are regressing.

> *In the factory we make cosmetics;*
> *in the drugstore we sell hope.*
>
> Charles Revson (1906-1975)
> Founder, Revlon
>
> *I think American salesmanship can be a weapon more powerful than the atomic bomb.*
>
> Henry J. Kaiser (1882-1967)
> Industrialist

If others are buying something that is newer and better than what you have, you will be losing ground to them if you don't upgrade, too. Your abandonment of a perfectly good item for the sake of competing with others becomes irrelevant. Because we are a very competitive culture, it is easy to sell people on the basis of comparison to others.

Consumer spending now accounts for two-thirds of our economy, which is good in the sense that a healthy level of consumer spending leads to a growing economy. Unfortunately, a lot of consumer spending is financed with debt for things that people merely want but don't need. When a corporation borrows money, it is typically to improve production and distribution or for other efficiencies that will increase revenues by more than enough to pay off the debt. Corporations borrow money for items that will make them richer; consumers borrow money for items that will make them poorer.

Even if advertising isn't stimulating you to make unnecessary purchases, the same can't be said for your neighbors. If the people around you are buying items because they are being persuaded by advertising, you may become a peripheral casualty. The commercials for a new car may not have much of an impact on you, but that new car in your neighbor's driveway might just do the trick. The car may not appeal to you in a commercial, but looking at your neighbor's new car and then looking at that comparative hunk-o'-junk in your driveway might just become too much to bear after a while.

Thousands upon thousands are yearly brought into a state of real poverty by their great anxiety not to be thought poor.

William Corbett (1942-)
Poet, Essayist

Never keep up with Joneses: drag them down to your level. It's cheaper.

Quentin Crisp (1908-1999)
English Raconteur

When you ask people who grew up during the Great Depression what it was like to be poor, a typical response is, "We were poor, but since everyone else was poor, we really didn't think of ourselves as poor." Such a response demonstrates that we judge our financial condition in relative terms. Our financial condition should be judged in absolute terms. One is either rich or poor, regardless of what others have.

Status, unlike financial condition, is judged totally relative to others. Our problem is that we have intertwined financial condition and status to the point where we cannot distinguish between the two. People in the Great Depression were poor, but they didn't feel they were because everyone else was poor, too. People today are rich, at least compared to the people in the Great Depression and to much of the world today. We don't feel rich because we see that most people have as much as we do, and many have a lot more. Our financial condition is good, but our status is low, so we believe that our financial condition is low, too. Such beliefs trigger dissatisfaction and a desire to climb the status ladder, which too often leads to financial trouble.

If there is a need to compare one's financial position, such comparisons should be made to one's own previous financial position, rather than making comparisons to someone else. The best way to make such a comparison is to look at one's personal balance sheet. The balance sheet totals all the assets and subtracts all the liabilities to determine a person's net worth. If the net worth is climbing over time, that's all that matters. An effective, albeit unglamorous, way to improve one's balance sheet is to pay down debt, which reduces liabilities. The balance sheet is the most important status symbol to those millionaires next door. They know that a solid balance sheet provides true status, not the bogus kind that comes from a Mercedes in the garage.

Too many people spend money they haven't earned,
to buy things they don't want,
to impress people they don't like.

Will Smith (1968-)
Actor, Musician

When people focus on external status instead of internal security, they end up with neither status nor security. The money that is devoted to impressing others is no longer available to strengthen the personal balance sheet.

There are consequences beyond the financial, too. The people who are impressed by cars, jewelry, or clothes are not worth anyone's time or attention, and they certainly aren't worth blowing good money in an effort to impress. What is worse, when someone blows good money in that manner, that person becomes someone impressive in an unintended manner. To impress means to affect or influence deeply, which can mean in a positive or a negative way. Anyone worth impressing in a positive way would only be impressed in a negative way by someone seeking status through spending. The people worth impressing are impressed by what others gave, not by what they got.

Wall Street is the only place that people ride to in a Rolls Royce to get advice from those who take the subway.

Warren Buffett (1930-)
Investor, Philanthropist

The more someone is the real deal about anything, the less it is necessary to publicize their authenticity. Let's compare two well-known billionaires, Warren Buffett and Donald Trump. Buffett is known for his wealth, but in recent years he has become known for giving his wealth away. His net worth in 2011 is estimated at $46 billion, and he has already given approximately $10 billion to charity. Warren Buffett lives in a 6,000 square-foot house in Omaha that he bought in 1958 for $31,500.

Donald Trump is known for... being Donald Trump. Trump's net worth is estimated to be $2.3 billion - considerably less than Buffett, though still a healthy sum. Trump's two main residences are his 30,000 square-foot apartment atop the Trump Tower in Manhattan and Mar-a-Lago, a 110,000 square-foot estate home in Florida.

As for his charitable nature, over the last twenty years, Trump's charitable contributions total approximately $4 million, all provided through the Donald J. Trump Foundation. Donald Trump's net worth is 1/20th of Warren Buffett's; his charitable contributions are 1/2,500th of Buffett's.

Both men are very smart and very successful. Buffett has never been obsessed with wealth and certainly not with the trappings of wealth. The same cannot be said for Trump. In 1991, Buffett spoke of Donald Trump and the perils of leverage. At that time, Trump had an estimated $2.5 billion in assets and $3.5 billion in liabilities. (Trump has filed three corporate bankruptcies since 1991.) Buffett said, "I would suggest that the big successes I've met had a fair amount of Ben Franklin in them. And Donald Trump did not." Not coincidentally, Ben Franklin and Warren Buffett are quoted in this book more than anyone else; there are no quotes from Trump.

Unfortunately, the image most people have of the super-wealthy is closer to Donald Trump than Warren Buffett, though Buffett more accurately personifies that group. Such misperceptions are understandable based simply on the difference in the way each man interacts with the media. Warren Buffett may want people to emulate him, especially regarding charitable giving, but he doesn't promote himself in any way. Donald Trump seeks media exposure to promote himself because he wants people to envy him. Such envy is the basis for class warfare and the desire to see the rich brought low.

> *People who have little thought of the relations of the rich to the poor generally assume that all that is necessary is for the rich to give to the poor, or that they should be compelled to give part of their wealth, and all would be well. But this is a great mistake.*
>
> Leo Tolstoy (1828-1910)
> Russian Novelist

It has been speculated that if the wealth of the richest five percent of Americans was given to the poorest five percent, within five years the richest would have all the wealth back. Such speculation does not mean that the wealthy are clever crooks or that the poor are incompetent dolts. What it is does mean is that the wealthy got that way because they know how to make and preserve wealth; the poor do not. What the poor don't know about money is the main reason they remain poor. Giving them money will not make them smarter about money, which is the first and most necessary step in fighting poverty.

Nothing is more cruel than giving someone a taste of something they crave, then denying it to them. Transfers of money from rich to poor in large amounts do not teach the poor how to use money wisely; it actually only encourages misuse of money. The best way to alleviate poverty on a large scale is to make sure that everyone in the society, starting in grade school, learns how wealth is really created and preserved and learns how people go about creating their own wealth, rather than looking to transfer it from someone else.

> *We should be careful to get out of an experience all the wisdom that is in it – not like the cat that sits down on a hot stove lid. She will never sit down on a hot stove lid again – and that is well; but also she will never sit down on a cold one anymore.*
>
> Mark Twain (1835-1910)
> Author, Humorist

How many times do we get burned by our investments? More important, why do we get burned more than once? Are we not learning from our own experiences? Are there forces at work conspiring to continuously trick us into making mistakes with our money?

If someone is getting burned on investments more than once, it isn't likely a vast conspiracy; it's more likely an inability to tell what is hot and cold.

Let's use Twain's cat analogy. The cat gets burned on a hot stove lid and avoids all stove lids in the future. Such an overreaction is like getting burned by investing in certain stocks and then forsaking all stocks forevermore. Stocks run hot and cold, just like stove lids. The trick is to test to see if they are hot or cold before you pick them up. Testing can be done with some simple analytical tools and an absence of emotion.

Getting burned more than once also involves another blind spot. This blind spot is not recognizing that stove lids aren't the only things that can burn you. There are people out there who got burned on tech stocks because everyone was buying them. They then moved into real estate because everyone was buying it. They then moved into gold because... well, you know. These people keep getting burned because they are following others who have already heated up that investment before it ever gets into their hands.

It isn't just the investments that can run hot and cold. The heat of the investment is actually directly related to the heat of the investors. Investments are inert - they do not generate their own heat. That heat comes from the people who keep touching and rubbing them. One of the best ways to keep from being burned on an investment is to see how hot the people who are touting it are. If they are unusually hot about something, the chances are extremely high you will get burned if you touch it.

We all know the investment axiom of buy low and sell high. We don't always know what constitutes high and low, however. Perhaps a better axiom, and one in line with our analogy here is - buy cold and sell hot. If you pick up an investment that is cold, it means that others haven't been rubbing and touching it much lately, and you won't get burned by lifting it. You can also then detect when that investment goes from cold to warm to hot, and you will unload it when it gets too hot to hold. You will know this in large part because you picked it up when it was cold, so you know how cold it can become again.

I find television very educational.
Every time somebody turns on the set,
I go into another room and read a book.

Groucho Marx (1890-1977)
Comedian

If television encouraged us to work as much as it encourages us to do everything else, we could better afford to buy more of everything it advertises.

Cullen Hightower (1923-)
Writer

Television, the hardware, may be the greatest invention of all time. Television, the software, is another story. The ability to have a device in your home that enables you to watch hundreds of different programs at any time and to watch events unfold in real time from around the world is truly amazing.

Because you can choose among hundreds of shows to watch at any given time, you know there is a lot of crap on at any given time, too. People may say that this was not a problem in the Golden Age of Television; although, when there were only three channels and three hours of prime time television each night, shows like *My Mother the Car* and *The Flying Nun* still managed to slip past the net.

> *The one function that TV news performs very well is that when there is no news we give it to you with the same emphasis as if there were.*
>
> David Brinkley (1920-2003)
> Newscaster
>
> *Television has a real problem. They have no page two. Consequently every big story gets the same play and comes across to the viewer as a really big, scary one.*
>
> Art Buchwald (1925-2007)
> Author, Journalist

There are certainly bad movies, music, and books, too. Many of these end up in one form or another as bad television. It is easier to avoid bad books, movies, and even music than it is to avoid bad television. When you arrange the main room in your house around the television, and you then spend several hours a day staring at it, you are going to be affected by what you are watching, for better or worse.

Forty years ago, the only financial information you got from television was a brief report on the local news about what the local stocks had done that day and Walter or David or Chet telling you on the network news what the Dow did, right before going to commercial break. With limited air time for news, financial news had to qualify as real news to get on the air.

Today there are at least four channels that broadcast financial and business news 24/7. Even if you have no interest in watching those channels, the regular news channels, of which there are even more, keep a running tab on the stock market throughout the day. There are also regular stories on those networks about what is going on in the financial world. CNN gives more air time in an hour to financial news than CBS gave to it in a week in the 1960's.

Assuming you still read a newspaper, the financial news in the paper is usually in the back of the paper and is simple and straightforward. You can see how the markets did and which companies made news, but everything is quite low key. The purpose of this news is to inform, not to excite.

The same cannot be said for financial news on TV. The cable news channels, as well as the financial news channels, are in a fight-to-the-death for ratings, which translates into advertising dollars. They know that informing their audience isn't enough to get them watching and keep them there. As a result, every bit of news is broadcast as though the fate of the world hangs in the balance. Bright colors, high definition, multiple boxes, and crawlers on the screen only add to the illusion that whatever they are telling you is vitally important to you and your portfolio.

What is good for these purveyors of news is bad for the consumers of that news. The ever-increasing volatility of markets has nothing to do with world events and everything to do with how those events (and non-events) are being reported. When an event is reported in such a sensationalistic way that action on the viewer's part is strongly implied, if not overtly stated, viewers will frequently swallow the bait and take some action that will have damaging effects on their long-term financial security. When it comes to creating long-term financial success, you might, in certain circumstances, respond to events; you don't react to them. TV prompts its viewers into reacting, rather than responding (or not), which disserves the audience it purports to serve.

Beware lest you lose the substance
by grasping at the shadow.

Aesop (620-564 BC)
Greek Writer

All media exist to invest our lives with
artificial perceptions and arbitrary values.

Marshall McLuhan (1911-1980)
Canadian Scholar

Television news can be so impactful that it can be hard to remember that what we are shown and told may not be how it is. As long as humans provide the programming, that programming will have some biases and will serve the interests of the media over the interests of its audience. If we get all our news and information from television, and especially if we get it from just one channel, we risk becoming parrots spouting another's point of view, rather than well-informed discerning observers of events.

> *Men are not against you; they're merely for themselves.*
> Gene Fowler (1890-1960)
> Journalist, Author

It's fairly easy to spot someone who is against you. Subtlety is not a trait most Americans possess. We can also assume that people are acting in their own self-interest, even when they are acting in a way that benefits others.

Selfishness and self-interest are not the same thing. Everyone who acts selfishly is acting in self-interest, but not everyone who acts in self-interest is acting selfishly. For example, people go to work every day to earn money, which is acting in their self-interest. Work becomes selfish only when rules or norms get violated, such as when an employee steals or takes credit for the work of another.

Just because people act in their own self-interest, it doesn't mean that their actions can't benefit others. Human interactions mimic biology in that they can be classified similarly. **Mutualism** is a relationship that benefits both parties. Most people seek such relationships because they form the best foundation for long-term benefits. **Commensalism** is a relationship where one party benefits while the other party is unaffected. In biology, this relationship is fine with both parties. In human relationships, commensalism can lead to resentment by the "unaffected" party, who can begin to feel exploited.

Commensalism can be confused with **parasitism,** which is a relationship where one party benefits while the other party is harmed. Such relationships are initiated by the parasite, and these are the relationships we need to fear. When it comes to parasites, it's OK to be a little paranoid.

Finally, there is **amensalism**, where one party is harmed while the other party is unaffected. The laws of unintended consequences come into play here. For example, the push to convert corn into ethanol had little effect on our consumption of foreign oil. However, the shifting of corn from food to fuel has led to increases in the price of many different types of food all over the world, especially in the poorer nations. In amensalism, one party is harmed by a party that does not benefit and is oblivious to the harm they are causing.

The goal in relationships should always be mutualism. Mutualism always provides the most benefits to either party over time. Commensalism is acceptable in small doses, but only if there is reciprocity, and soon. Parasitism is to be avoided, but it has to be avoided by the host; the parasite has every incentive to have such a relationship. Amensalism occurs when the unaffected party doesn't pay enough attention to the condition of the affected party, and the affected party doesn't speak up. When someone is standing on your foot, it doesn't benefit either of you if you keep quiet about it.

> *Sometimes one pays most for the things that one gets for nothing.*
>
> Albert Einstein (1879-1955)
> Theoretical physicist

Everyone is tempted by the free lunch. Seniors are invited to a free meal if they are willing to listen to someone talk about protecting their nest egg in retirement. Before they can get out of the room, those seniors get pummeled with a sales pitch about investing in annuities, gold, or whatever the "host" is peddling that day. Even the mosquito that's looking for a quick snack often finds itself on the receiving end of a fatal swat if it takes too much or takes too long.

It's never something for nothing; it's only something for nothing **now**. When you buy something on credit, you are getting something for nothing now, but at least you know that you will pay later and how much you will pay. The something-for-nothing ploy has you paying later, but the terms are unknown. The payment may be in money, but it can also be in time and aggravation.

If you remember that people always act in self-interest, it is easier to be more alert to something-for-nothing deals. If someone can make parasitism look like altruism, it becomes a lot easier to establish a relationship. If someone can make it look like they are giving rather than taking, the victim will invite the relationship and will remain unaware of the parasitism far longer than otherwise. The best cons work that way - by doing the mark a favor - giving something for nothing - they can then bleed the victim dry.

We should aim rather at leveling down our desires than leveling up our means.

Aristotle (384-322 BC)
Greek Philosopher

Lord, grant that I may always desire more than I can accomplish.

Michelangelo (1475-1564)
Italian Artist

Humans desire many things, but at or near the top of any list would be material wealth and personal accomplishment. The two are often interrelated. Some people strive for accomplishment as a way to material wealth. Some people believe that material wealth is an accomplishment in itself, regardless of how it is acquired. Some people use material wealth to enable personal accomplishments that might otherwise be unattainable, and some people seek personal accomplishment without any regard to the material cost or reward that their pursuit might entail.

The most noble personal accomplishments are those that have no connection to material wealth and are not motivated by the desire to be recognized by others. People who work in anonymity to achieve a goal, typically a goal that will benefit others, would fall into this category. Examples might include volunteers working to eradicate a disease or someone training to complete a marathon for the first time. In this category, you are only trying to impress yourself, even if your accomplishment will benefit others.

Some people accomplish great things for less than great reasons. Actors, musicians, and athletes who perform their craft well, but are motivated by the desire for fame and fortune would be examples. For these people, fame and fortune are the cause and expertise in their profession is the effect. Ideally, expertise in one's profession should be the cause, with fame and fortune the effect.

Some people see material wealth as an accomplishment worthy of whatever sacrifices are necessary to achieve it. Many of the CEOs responsible for creating the financial crisis in recent years would fall into this category, as would Mafia kingpins and everyone else who doesn't care about the damage they inflict in the course of reaching their goal.

Some people will use material wealth to accomplish goals that were previously unattainable. Bill Gates is using his wealth to lead the final push to eradicate polio in the world. His vast wealth makes it possible for him to make such an accomplishment possible. Such an accomplishment never entered Gates' head until he had accumulated the financial resources to make it happen.

Almost everyone desires fame and fortune because they symbolize personal accomplishment. That desire can motivate people to accomplish some great things. The problem with that kind of external motivation is that once the fame and fortune are achieved, there can be a hollowness to them. The accomplishments that a person pursues because it will help others and/or because it will make that individual a better person are the accomplishments that are most rewarding when they are finally accomplished.

> *There is a vast difference between success at twenty-five and success at sixty. At sixty, nobody envies you. Instead, everybody rejoices generously, sincerely, in your good fortune.*
>
> Marie Dressler (1868-1934)
> Canadian Actress

How others react to our success can greatly affect our reaction to that success. There will always be people who are envious of others' success, and we have to ignore them if we are going to accomplish anything in life. People applaud success they feel is deserved, which is one reason why success at sixty is applauded more than success at twenty-five. Every year at graduation time, there will be a story about someone in their eighties or nineties who is finally graduating high school. It's the kind of story that makes everyone feel good because no one believes an octogenarian didn't earn that diploma. An eighteen-year-old who accomplishes the same thing with six decades less experience doesn't get recognized for the same accomplishment, largely because if someone accomplishes something at a young age, we tend to think it is the result of luck or God-given talent. Success at an early age can be difficult to deal with under the best of circumstances. When others question the validity of that success, merely because it came early in life, the individual can begin to question their own worthiness.

> *Too many people overvalue what they are not and undervalue what they are.*
>
> Malcolm Forbes (1919-1990)
> Publisher, Forbes Magazine

To expand on the preceding quote, we also overvalue what we don't have and undervalue what we do. We see what others have, and we become envious, while not caring for and appreciating what we already have. We let others dictate our feelings about our own station in life. We cede control of our well-being to strangers.

Before we let others manipulate us that way, it might help to remember that most of them have become misguided by our culture, and a lot of them are just plain morons. Give yourself credit for knowing what is really important in life, and it will be easier to tune out the droning from the herd.

A LIVING & A LIFETIME

From conception to cremation, no other human invention influences our lives like money.

Have you ever wondered how much thought you were given? I'm referring to how much thought your parents gave to you before they created you. Some parents plan for years before they have a child. For some, it comes as a pleasant surprise. For some, sadly, it comes as an unpleasant surprise.

Before having a child, there are many thoughts to be thought. Are the parents ready to take on that responsibility? Are there health risks to having a baby? In what kind of world will that child grow up? Who else can be depended on to help when needed? What are the costs involved?

That last question, if it could be accurately answered prior to conception, would cause many prospective parents to reconsider. The USDA provides data on costs to raise a child from birth to age eighteen. For a low-income family, the annual cost for one child is about $11,000; for a middle-income family, about $15,000; for an upper-income family, about $25,000. The cost-per-child drops as more children are added, due to economies of scale and less money to spend per child.

As sobering as those figures are, they do not take into effect two other expenses - inflation and higher education. The above figures are from 2010. Even if inflation averages less than 3% during the eighteen years of a child's minority, the total cost to get a child through high school is over $200,000 for a low-income family, almost $300,000 for a middle-income family, and nearly $500,000 for an upper-income family.

The above figures only go as far as high school graduation. If the child goes on to earn a Bachelor's Degree, that cost is currently in the $100,000 to $200,000 range. For a child born today, that figure will double or triple by the time he/she gets to college.

For a lower-income family, a child can cost more than $200,000, even if they are just getting by now. For an upper-income family (over $100,000 per year), they could be looking at expenses totaling nearly a million dollars by the time the parental obligation ceases. Unless the potential parents are serious about wanting to become parents, their best investment would be in contraceptives.

> *My hair stands on end at the cost and charges of these boys. Why was I ever a father! Why was my father ever a father!*
>
> Charles Dickens (1812-1870)
> English Novelist

For thousands of years, the only security people could hope for in their old age (assuming they even lived that long) was their children. There were no methods to accumulate wealth, save for retirement, or insure proper care at the onset of old age. Since it was impossible for all but lords and such to finance their own care in old age, the next best thing was to have several children, with the expectation that at least one of them would live long enough to provide the necessary care in old age. Until the last hundred years or so, one's social security was in the form of one's progeny.

With the advent of Social Security, pensions, 401(k)'s, and long-term care insurance, people no longer need children to be assured of support when they can no longer earn a living. One reason for declining birth rates in all the developed countries is that the motivation for having children has shifted from need to want. In these countries, people want children for the sake of having children. In the less developed countries, children are still the source of old age security, and birth rates in those countries remain high.

It is a testament to the instinctive drive to keep our species going that we keep having children. We certainly have the means to easily prevent conception. There is generally no financial incentive to have children. They may be a tax deduction, but if a couple making $150,000 per year raises two children, the money they would spend on those children could have grown into $7-10 million if it were invested at 7% and withdrawals began at age 70. It is unlikely that any child, no matter how successful, could support Mom and Dad in the same style that $7-10 million could. These figures do not include any lost income that might occur if a parent should leave the workforce to care for the children.

In Japan and many European countries, people are looking at such numbers and deciding that the cost of parenthood is too high. As a result, the populations in these countries are in decline or, at best, they are being propped up by immigrants from developing countries. Declining populations have negative long-term ramifications, as both the labor force and domestic markets will also shrink in the future.

> *Children sweeten labours,*
> *but they make misfortunes more bitter.*
>
> Sir Francis Bacon (1561-1626)
> English Philosoper, Statesman

Fortunately, the U.S. has maintained a healthy population growth, fueled by both immigration and a healthy birth rate among the citizenry. Even though Americans are aware of the high cost of raising children, we also recognize the long-term benefits to our nation to maintain a balance in our population. More important, we also know that the joy of raising children is worth all the sacrifices, including sizeable financial ones.

Money is becoming a larger factor in our lives before our lives even begin. Paradoxically, the people who can most afford children are the ones looking closest at the numbers and having the fewest children. Birth rates are still higher at the lower income levels, even though it is a greater struggle to meet the financial demands of parenthood. Money not only determines the quality of life, but also whether a life will even be created in many cases.

> *It is the mind that makes the body rich.*
> William Shakespeare (1564-1616)
> English Playwright

The first glimpse of what life is like for adults occurs the day a child first goes to school. For the first time, a child's routine mimics the parents' - they have to get up, get ready, and be at a specific place at a specific time to spend the day completing tasks that are set by others. Those others will also evaluate the child's performance; and promotions, praise and punishments will be meted out based on the quality of the effort and the performance.

The national average spending per-student per-year is currently around $10,000. The U.S. ranks in the top five in per-student spending; the only ones who spend more are a handful of small developed countries in northern Europe. The figures vary widely by state, though. New York is at or near the top, spending 70% above the national average. Utah is at or near the bottom, spending less than 60% of the national average, or less than one-third the per-pupil spending of New York. Despite the disparity in per-student spending, Utah has a higher high school graduation rate than New York.

The lesson to be learned from these numbers is that, while money is a vital ingredient in a good education, it is only one of many factors that determine how well our children are learning.

> *If a man empties his purse into his head,*
> *no one can take it from him.*
> *An investment in knowledge pays the best interest.*
> Benjamin Franklin (1706-1790)
> Founding Father

By the time a student graduates from high school, his/her education will have already cost from $60,000 to $200,000. These figures are for public schools; private schools can run much higher. If a student plans to go to college, the numbers really start to climb. The average state college costs about $8,000 per year in tuition and fees, while the average private college averages about $28,000, so a Bachelor's Degree can cost from $32,000 to over $100,000 in most cases. The final tab for all this education ranges from about $100,000 to over $300,000.

Is it worth it? According the U.S. Census Bureau, it probably is. On average, high school graduates can expect over their lifetime to earn $1.2 million; those with a Bachelor's Degree, $2.1 million; a Master's Degree, $2.5 million; a Ph.D., $3.4 million; and those with a professional degree, $4.4 million. Annual salary differentials may be even greater, as more years in school mean fewer years at work.

> *Formal education will make you a living;*
> *self-education will make you a fortune.*
> Jim Rohn (1930-2009)
> Motivational Speaker

Although the data support formal education as a source of greater **income** potential, our formal education system cannot claim credit for making Americans **wealthier.** Almost nowhere in America's formal education system is there any instruction on financial planning, money management, wealth creation, or any other topic related to what we should do with money once we possess some of it.

There are some theories as to the reasons for our reluctance to teach our children about money in school. I believe that one major reason has to do with the mindset of educators. People who go into education do not do so for the money. As a group, they are not motivated by money, but by what they believe are higher ideals. There can be a tendency to think of any financial education as submission to the powers of capitalism, materialism, and the almighty dollar. The result of this collective mindset is that financial education is considered less worthy of attention compared to traditional subjects like math or social studies.

There is a contradiction in such thinking. The main reason people spend hundreds of thousands of dollars to educate their children is to enable them to get good jobs. What is the definition of a good job? There are many factors to consider, but the most universally agreed upon feature of a good job is a high income. What is the purpose of a high income? One purpose is to live well in the present, but the most important purpose of a high income is to build wealth for the future. In summation, the most important reason people have to spend great sums on formal education is to increase their ability to create wealth. Wouldn't it be more effective to actually teach people the proper ways to create wealth, rather than merely teaching them how to get a job that will pay more and hoping that when they get that money they might somehow figure out how to keep some of it?

> *Nothing is really work unless you would rather be doing something else.*
>
> James M. Barrie (1860-1937)
> Scottish Author

Once students graduate, other issues surface. First, it is likely if they have graduated college that they are in debt, and the meter begins running to pay back college loans right after graduation. It doesn't matter if they are unemployed, either. The ease of obtaining loans of all kinds in college (due in large part to the safety net of the parents) now comes back to haunt these graduates when they discover how much and for how long they will be paying every month to clear these debts. In 2010, the **average** student loan debt was $25,000. As tuitions continue to rise faster than the inflation rate, the average debt will rise even faster.

Another issue that new graduates face is the lack of training to quickly assume the duties of most of the jobs they will acquire. Most jobs have specific skills that are often taught after a person is hired. The need to begin an intense training program right out of college can be depressing for recent graduates. They can begin to question the value of their education and why they needed a four-year degree simply to be eligible to get a job that requires still more intense learning.

While new graduates dream of beginning a successful and fulfilling career, most of them have to settle for getting a job, at least right out of school. Many people spend their twenties finding out the careers they **don't** want to have. There is a lot of trial and error in the early stages of one's working life, but that is usually necessary to find out what that person can do and wants to do.

> *The test of a vocation is the love of the drudgery it involves.*
>
> Logan Pearsall Smith (1865-1946)
> Essayist

In the early years of a working life, it's hard to plan for the future. Wages are low; debts can be high; households are being established, and the future consists of getting set up for a promotion or investigating a better job elsewhere. As a result, valuable time gets lost in planning for the future, and the longed-for promotion that can offset the procrastination rarely happens as planned.

Many careers have long apprenticeships that follow many years of formal education. Fewer doctors and lawyers would endure the grueling early years of their careers if they hadn't already put so much time and expense into it. Such a high expense in time and money can force people to remain in careers for which they are not suited.

The early years of one's career are the high effort/low reward years. Those who change careers frequently may find they never reach the low effort/high reward years. When people talk about paying one's dues, they typically refer to paying those dues within a specific career. Getting transfer credits in a career can be like getting transfer credits in college; the place a person is transferring into decides what credits will be accepted from prior places.

> *Profit is a byproduct of work;*
> *happiness is its chief product.*
>
> Henry Ford (1863-1947)
> Founder, Ford Motor Company
>
> *The best augury of a man's success in his profession*
> *is that he thinks it is the finest in the world.*
>
> George Eliot (1819-1880)
> English Novelist

Few of us have any choice of whether or not we will work. Even those who have the option not to work choose to work when they enjoy what they do. Since few of us have the option not to work, we should at least attempt to find the type of work that can fill our spirits as well as our wallets.

Many people end up gravitating into careers they don't particularly like because, at certain points in their careers, they took a job that paid more without giving equal consideration to their affinity for the job. This short-term desire for higher pay very often ends up costing more in the long run. To be among the best in any profession requires skill, experience, and also a love of the work. In a great many career fields, the top 10% make 50% of the money. The top 10% don't get there without having a love for the work they do. It can be more lucrative to forego short-term raises in a job you dislike to pursue long-term success in a job you love.

Working at a job you dislike is still preferable to unemployment, which many people don't believe when they are working at such jobs. However, the people who dislike their jobs are typically the first ones to be let go, in part because their attitude affects their performance in a negative way. Once they become unemployed, they soon realize how important their old job was to them. Like the song says, you don't know what you got 'til it's gone, and that's especially true of a job that provides you with, not just a paycheck, but also stability, security, and the pride of contributing to, rather than taking from, society. During times of high unemployment, job dissatisfaction may actually increase, as everyone is working harder. However, complaints are fewer because alternatives are, too.

Work banishes those three great evils, boredom, vice and poverty.

Voltaire (1694-1778)
French Writer, Philosopher

He that never labors may know the pains of idleness, but not the pleasures.

Samuel Johnson (1709-1784)
English Poet, Essayist

Because there is so much emphasis on formal education today, and by formal I mean a Bachelor's Degree and higher, too many young people are finding themselves unemployed or underemployed. The reasons go beyond a slow economy.

As our economy has moved from manufacturing into services, we have stopped encouraging young people to get into "the trades." We have been led to believe that only those with a Bachelor's Degree (or more) can earn a decent living. While the statistics presented earlier bear that out for the population as a whole, it does not mean that it applies on an individual basis.

How many parents in the U.S. who have the ability to send their children to a four-year college have encouraged them to look at alternatives? Very few, probably. Many more parents have given their children no option but to go to college, even when those children show little interest in higher education.

These children go off and earn degrees in art history or political science or philosophy, then end up working the next five years stacking slacks at The Gap. Meanwhile, a high school classmate who didn't have the same options went to trade school and became a plumber, where he now charges $75 an hour and will soon be starting his own business. At their twentieth high school reunion, the college graduate is stuck in a lower-management position that isn't fulfilling spiritually or financially, while the plumber has two-hundred employees and a second home at the lake.

> *The best investment is in the tools of one's own trade.*
> Benjamin Franklin (1706-1790)
> Founding Father

Higher education has become too expensive to ignore the cost-benefit relationship. The census figures regarding lifetime earnings at various education levels assume that everyone in those groups is otherwise equal in areas like intelligence and initiative. If someone has the intelligence and discipline to earn a Master's Degree, it is unlikely that same person, if only limited to a high school diploma, would only earn the average lifetime income for high school graduates. That person would likely need to be self-employed to make a good living without higher education, but it is entirely possible that such a person could make even more money without a degree than with one. The biggest factor in determining career success is not education, but the innate talents and work ethic of the individual.

Before spending six figures on a college degree, it's important to assess how that degree will affect that individual's earning potential. Going to college has become too expensive to think of it in terms of a "life experience." Whether someone goes to college needs to be analyzed from the perspective of return on investment. If the case can be made that such an investment in time and money will generate a sufficient return, then go for it. Otherwise, for an investment of four years and a hundred grand, there are far more rewarding "life experiences" to be had.

> *It is not the employer who pays the wages.*
> *Employers only handle the money.*
> *It is the customer who pays the wages.*
> Henry Ford (1863-1947)
> Founder, Ford Motor Company
>
> *If you mean to profit, learn to please.*
> Winston Churchill (1874-1965)
> British Prime Minister

Regardless of whether you become a doctor, a business owner, or a fry cook at McDonalds, your success will ultimately be measured by how your customers perceive the quality of your work. Talent, degrees, and even celebrity will not protect you from the judgment of the people who are served by your work. The best businesses recognize that shareholder satisfaction and employee satisfaction are the direct result of customer satisfaction.

Many people work in jobs where they don't have direct contact with customers; that is irrelevant. The assembly line worker is far from the customer, but if the quality of that person's work is substandard, it will show up in the product. Customer complaints and lost sales will be noticed by management, who will seek the source of the problem. They will find it soon enough, and if the worker is at fault, the worker will soon be out of work.

Unless the job means more than the pay
it will never pay more.

H. Bertram Lewis (1867-1944)
Businessman

Men who do things without being told
draw the most wages.

Edwin H. Stuart (1890-1968)
Businessman

Everyone who has ever uttered the phrase, "It's not my job" to a boss has probably done more harm to his/her career than they realize. Those words can be like fingernails on a blackboard to an employer, and they never forget those who utter them.

Part of the blame for such an employee attitude can be placed on the job description. Employers create job descriptions so that employees can be held accountable for performing the duties listed in that job description. The implication, though, is that the stated duties are the only duties for which the employee is responsible. When the employer set a floor of expectations regarding what an employee is to do, they unknowingly also set a ceiling on what they could expect an employee to do. Unions will codify this ceiling into labor contracts, which don't merely discourage, but may expressly forbid, an employee doing work outside of specified duties.

When employers get too specific on job duties, they stifle initiative. When employees assume that a task is not their job, they demonstrate a lack of initiative. Initiative is the hormones of any enterprise. Initiative is more abundant in smaller, newer enterprises because there are many things to be done and too few people to do them. Saying "It's not my job." in these organizations doesn't work because everyone is doing everything that needs to be done to make the business successful. When organizations become large and bureaucratic, job duties get more specific; every task is expected to be assigned in a job description, and employees are less likely to show initiative by performing additional duties.

They copied all they could copy,
But they couldn't copy my mind;
And I left them sweatin' and stealin',
A year and a half behind.

Rudyard Kipling (1865-1935)
English Poet, Novelist

Every organization needs to make sure they have a culture in place that encourages employees to make suggestions, to offer improvements, to improve efficiencies and customer service without fear that they will be criticized for overstepping their responsibilities. Employees, for their part, need to look for ways to do all the above, even if management isn't initially receptive. Any organization that stifles employee initiative is not a place that any employee with initiative should want to remain. The employee is better off using that initiative to find a workplace where its use is encouraged and rewarded.

> *Any use of a human being in which less is demanded of him and less is attributed to him than his full status is a degradation and a waste.*
>
> Norbert Wiener (1894-1964)
> Mathematician

If people truly believe in the mission of the organization that employs them, they should want to do everything within their power to help that organization accomplish that mission. If that means doing work that falls outside the normal day-to-day duties of their job, they should be willing to do them. Of course, no employer should ask any employee to do anything that violates an individual's ethics or the law. Employees should also know the difference between a good employer that is asking everyone for their best effort and an employer that exploits and abuses its employees.

If you are a boss and if you lost a good employee over a five percent pay raise from a new employer, you need to face a fact. The reason the employee left was not the raise - it was you.

Research has shown that it typically takes only a five percent raise to compel an unhappy employee to change employers, but it takes a twenty percent raise to compel a happy employee to change. When someone is happy in their work environment, their preference is to stay there, rather than take a risk by changing jobs. When workers aren't happy, they will assume that almost anyplace is better than where they are now, so it takes very little financial incentive to get the unhappy employee to move.

A good man likes a hard boss. I don't mean a nagging boss or a grouchy boss. I mean a boss who insists on things being done right and on time; a boss who is watching things closely enough so that he knows a good job from a poor one. Nothing is more discouraging to a good man than a boss who is not on the job, and who does not know whether things are going well or badly.
William Feather (1889-1981)
Publisher, Author

When people talk about bosses they held in high regard, a common description of them is "firm but fair." If a boss isn't firm, the slackers will slack, and the good workers will have to pick up that slack. If they aren't fair, anyone who isn't getting favored treatment is resentful.

The firm-but-fair boss is able to balance the concern for results (firm) and the concern for people (fair). It is more art than science, which is why truly great bosses can be rare. Great bosses can still be unappreciated by some workers. Those workers often end up losing their jobs and realize how good they had it only after they discover the flaws in their new boss.

To be firm but fair requires constant reassessing and recalibration. Both the needs of the employees and the needs of the organization are constantly changing. In tough economic times, it can be easy to assume that less attention should be given to the employees to focus more attention on the health of the organization. The attention a boss gives to the organization and the employees is not a fixed total, though. Greater attention to one should not come at the expense of the other. In fact, during tough economic times, a good boss ramps up attention to both the organization and the employees, who feel vulnerable during this period and need to know the boss has them covered. Great bosses are actually made during the tough times because they have to carry extra-heavy loads of firmness and fairness, while keeping them both balanced.

When we were in school, the one adjective we hoped would be ascribed to us was "popular." There was often recognition of the most popular students at the prom or in the yearbook; but something happened during the transition from school to work. Evaluations of popularity ceased. Instead of being lauded for being popular, we now had a new accolade to strive for - "competent."

> *There's a man in the world who is never turned down,*
> *Wherever he chances to stray;*
> *He gets the glad hand in the populous town,*
> *Or out where the farmers make hay;*
> *He's greeted with pleasure on deserts of sand,*
> *And deep in the aisles of the woods;*
> *Wherever he goes there's a welcoming hand –*
> *He's the man who delivers the goods.*
>
> Walt Whitman (1819-1892)
> Poet

In the workplace, the only person who might be classified as popular is likely a perky-but-competent low-level individual who isn't considered a threat to anyone. The popular person in the office may be universally liked, but no one aspires to be that person, at least not within the office environment. To be popular as we think about it generally requires that someone has no real responsibilities to others.

In the workplace, the only thing that matters is results. The only ones who will give you credit for your efforts are God and your parents. They care enough about you to look at your effort as well as your results; your employer and the world at large do not. Results are measurable, while effort is not. Results are also comparable, and the world uses them to see how you compare to your competition. The world is a very bottom-line place, and effort that does not translate into results does not help the bottom line. When your parents said that life isn't fair, this is one reality to which they were referring.

> *Every man should make up his mind that if he expects to succeed, he must give an honest return for the other man's dollar.*
>
> E.H. Harriman (1848-1909)
> Railroad Executive
>
> *A day's pay for a day's work is more than adequate when both the work and the pay are appreciated as much as they are expected.*
>
> Cullen Hightower (1923-)
> Writer

Whenever there is exchange between people, there is the possibility that one or even both parties will feel they have been exploited. As long as the market for exchanges is as free as possible, that possibility is lessened. If both parties are free to accept or decline an offer, the odds increase that the parties will eventually reach a deal that is satisfactory to both. When one party is compelled to accept a deal, you end up with a win-lose, rather than a win-win proposition.

When the auto unions held great power and foreign competition was insignificant, the auto companies agreed to compensation and benefit packages that became unsustainable with increased competition. The high labor costs compromised the ability to make a competitive car at a competitive price, and the result was bankruptcy for two of the big three U.S. automakers. The workers paid a high price, in that there are now far fewer auto workers making far less money than in the past.

> *The worst crime against working people is a company which fails to operate at a profit.*
>
> Samuel Gompers (1850-1924)
> Labor Union Leader

Profit is not about taking advantage of workers, which will cause a company to soon fail. Profit is not about enriching shareholders; although, shareholders are entitled to a reward commensurate with their risk. Profit is about supplying the company with the lifeblood to keep going. Without profit, a company cannot adapt and grow to successfully compete. Without profit, shareholders will find a better use for their money. Without profit, wages stagnate, and the best employees leave for greener pastures. Without profit, there is no point to it all.

If there is an adversarial relationship between employer and employees, that organization is doomed to fail. There are too many enemies from without for people to spend their resources fighting enemies from within. External forces often prompt organizations to resolve some internal disputes, but such solutions are rarely permanent.

Competition within an organization is good, unless it creates an adversarial relationship. There is always a certain adversarial relationship between labor and management. Competition occurs between similar individuals or groups working toward a particular goal. If there is competition to improve efficiency or increase sales, everyone benefits, as long as the efforts made are toward the goal. When competition becomes about beating the other guys, it can deteriorate into trying to make the others fail, rather than focusing on self-improvement.

> *Some see private enterprise as a predatory target to be shot, others as a cow to be milked, but few are those who see it as a sturdy horse pulling the wagon.*
>
> Winston Churchill (1874-1965)
> British Prime Minister

In 2010, federal government spending was more than 23% of GDP, the highest percentage since World War II. In extraordinary times, as in World War II and the Great Depression, the government spends more to stimulate the economy or to defend the nation. Even during the New Deal of the 1930's, federal spending rarely exceeded 10% of GDP. During normal periods since World War II, that percentage has hovered around 20%. Total government spending, which includes state and local governments, exceeded 40% of GDP in 2010 for the first time since the Civil War.

Why is this level of spending a problem? For starters, some 40% of government spending is in the form of borrowed funds. That level is simply not sustainable. Also, government spending is less efficient than business spending, because there is no profit motive. Less efficient spending results in fewer benefits to the economy from each dollar spent. Private enterprises spending money also generates more tax revenues than government spending of the same amount generates. When government takes money from private enterprise to spend, they actually hurt their own revenue stream in the future.

Never stand begging for that which
you have the power to earn.

Miguel de Cervantes (1547-1616)
Spanish Novelist, Poet

A person who can acquire no property,
can have no other interest but to eat as much,
and to labor as little as possible.

Adam Smith (1723-1790)
Scottish Philosopher, Economist

Private enterprise is the best means yet devised to enable people to earn a living and acquire property. Only private enterprises create property, which is synonymous with wealth. That wealth also enables wages to be paid, creating future wealth.

> *It is not from the benevolence of the butcher, the brewer, or the baker, that we expect our dinner, but from their regard to their own interest.*
>
> Adam Smith (1723-1790)
> Scottish Philosopher, Economist

Quid pro quo is a Latin phrase we often hear used in legal references. Its translation is **what for what**, which we further translate to mean a favor for a favor, give and take, and even tit for tat.

Quid pro quo is one manifestation of how people act in their own self-interest. Our economic system is based on the concept of quid pro quo. Every business that sells a product or service does so because they expect to be compensated financially. When customers are no longer able to pay, they are no longer customers. Quid pro quo and our entire economic system are based on the biological concept of mutualism that was discussed previously.

No one willingly makes a deal when they feel they are giving up more than they are getting. Since it is rare that both parties in any transaction feel that they traded exactly evenly, how do any deals ever get done?

Take the example of the butcher in the previous quote. The butcher has meat, but meat's usefulness as meat to the butcher diminishes as his belly gets full. Money is far more useful than meat, at least to the butcher, so he will gladly exchange meat he won't personally consume for a price. The customer is hungry, and since money is inedible, the customer is willing to exchange money for meat. The only thing left to be worked out is how much money for how much meat. The cost is determined by many factors, including the desperation of each party to make the exchange. The older the meat, the more desperate the butcher is to sell it and the less desperate the customer is to buy it.

It is in everyone's self-interest to have money, because money is the best tool to supply people with what they need and want. It is in everyone's interest to obtain that money by legitimate means because the consequences of getting money by illegitimate means are too serious for most of us to risk. It is, therefore, in everyone's interest to work in some way to legally provide goods or services for which others will pay a fair price.

But this I say. He which soweth sparingly shall reap also sparingly, and he which soweth bountifully shall reap also bountifully.

II Corinthians 9:6

We have no more right to consume happiness without producing it than to consume wealth without producing it.

George Bernard Shaw (1856-1950)
Irish Playwright

If you go to a pastry shop in many parts of Louisiana and order a dozen donuts, you will get your dozen. The proprietor will typically add a thirteenth donut and say, "Lagniappe." Lagniappe is a little extra something that a merchant gives a customer, as a way of generating goodwill.

If you've ever eaten at a restaurant where they bring a mint or a chocolate with your check, you may have gotten a couple of extras from your server, who will make a point to mention that they aren't supposed to do that, but you were really nice people! Naturally, you leave a nice tip and look forward to going back.

Giving more than expected, more than is your contractual obligation, is the best way to guarantee return business and long-term success. I doubt any pastry shop ever went bust because they offered an extra donut. Even if the server at the restaurant had to pay for the extra candies out of pocket, the extra tips and goodwill would more than cover it.

> *The more men, generally speaking, will do for a dollar when they make it, the more that dollar will do for them when they spend it.*
>
> William Boetcker (1873-1962)
> Presbyterian Minister

We think of money as something to invest, but we don't often think about our investment in money. Older people are often less willing to pay as much for certain items as younger people. Part of this reluctance may stem from different financial situations and different maturity levels regarding money. Part of it is also the perspective of the older person. If a seventy-year old can remember when a new Chevy cost $1,600, there will be a reluctance to spend ten to fifteen times that amount for a new Chevy today. The seventy-year old remembers how many hours' wages it took to save up the $1,600 back in 1960, and that person is mentally paying for a 2012 car with 1960 dollars.

Even when we become successful and make a lot of money, it's hard not to think back to the days when we were doing hard work for the minimum wage. Knowing how hard we had to work to make $100 back in the day makes it harder to spend $100 today, even if we only had to work an hour or less today to earn it. Such prudence can be a good thing, provided it doesn't keep us from enjoying any of the fruits of our labors.

> *He who will not economize will have to agonize.*
>
> Confucius (551-479 BC)
> Chinese Philosopher
>
> *Ask thy purse what thou should spend.*
>
> Scottish Proverb

Far worse than old people who don't spend money they could spend are young people who spend money they shouldn't spend. Generally speaking, if an old person has money, it was likely accumulated through a lifetime of prudent spending. Decades of habit can't just be turned off, especially when that person no longer earns an income and worries about the cost of living in old age.

Habits of thrift are uncommon in younger people,

for several reasons. Most grew up in relative affluence, and thrift was never instilled at an early age. If such habits aren't learned in one's youth, they aren't likely to be acquired once that person is working and earning a decent income for the first time. Younger people are also more susceptible to marketing messages, so the temptations to spend frivolously are greater. Finally, younger people don't picture themselves ever getting old, disabled, or even unemployed for an extended period. They see no compelling reason to be careful with money now because they can't picture a time when money won't be readily available.

One cannot both feast and become rich.

Ashanti Proverb

When prosperity comes, do not use all of it.

Confucius (551-479 BC)
Chinese Philosopher

By sowing frugality we reap liberty, a golden harvest.

Agesilaus (444-360 BC)
King of Sparta

There was a time when being called frugal was a compliment. Since World War II it has become something of an insult. One of the synonyms for frugal is **parsimonious**. Some of the synonyms for parsimonious are stingy, ungenerous, miserly, mean and tightfisted.

Frugality simply means avoiding unnecessary expenditures. It does not mean avoiding necessary expenditures or any expenditure where the benefit outweighs the cost. To be frugal means to take your money seriously. More people choose to do the opposite, to be frivolous with money, because it is more fun and less work to do so.

> *Economy is a distributive virtue, and consists not in saving but in selection. Parsimony requires no providence, no sagacity, no powers of combination, no comparison, no judgment.*
>
> Edmund Burke (1729-1797)
> Member, British Parliament

Frivolity involves a default answer of "Yes" to a purchase. Parsimony involves a default answer of "No" to a purchase. Frugality involves a default answer of "I'll think about it" to a purchase. A blanket Yes or No answer to a question is the easy way out. Thinking about it involves work, and as we know, work is the essential ingredient to creating wealth. Therefore, one of the surest ways to wealth is the practice of frugality.

> *Frugality includes all the other virtues.*
>
> Cicero (106-43 BC)
> Roman Statesman

There is nothing like a shortage to spur frugality. You may have had the experience of flying down the highway and discovering two things simultaneously: you were almost out of gas, and you were uncertain if you had enough to reach the next gas station. At that point you slowed down, turned off the A/C, and did everything you could to coax the maximum MPGs to avoid having to walk the last few miles to the gas station. Of course, once your tank was full again, you resumed your spendthrift driving habits.

> *Frugality is founded on the principle that all riches have limits.*
>
> Edmund Burke (1729-1797)
> Member, British Parliament

If you are young, if you have a good job with a bright future, if the economy is strong and you have few obligations, your income potential seems unlimited. During these times it would be easy to develop the habits of thrift because income is high and obligations are low, so one can be thrifty and still have an enjoyable lifestyle. Of course, in such a position, maybe one person in a hundred might show such self-control.

The Great Recession that began in 2007 is the first time most American workers have experienced a true financial crisis, both nationally and personally. They have realized for the first time that their income and wealth potential are limited. They have also become aware that valuable time has been lost in their efforts to increase income and accumulate wealth needed for retirement. Because many people did not internally impose frugality during the good times, they have had it imposed externally during the bad times.

For a great many Americans, they will never

again live the lifestyle they had before the Great Recession. Even if their incomes rebound completely, they will have to save more and spend less if they hope to have even a semblance of the retirement they thought was a certainty just a few years ago.

Psychologically, many have had their spendthrift ways kicked out of them, which is actually a good thing. The more severe the impact of the Great Recession is on a person or a family, the more likely they are to retain the lessons of frugality they've learned, even when the crisis has passed.

Economy does not consist in saving the coal, but in using the time while it burns.

Ralph Waldo Emerson (1803-1882)
Philosopher, Essayist

No gain is as certain as that which proceeds from the economical use of what you already have.

Latin Proverb

There is always the risk that hard times will create a population that becomes averse to any spending, even spending that is beneficial. Just as wasteful spending hinders the ability to build real wealth, hoarding money can also have the same effect. If you don't perform necessary maintenance on your home, you may not be spending money, but the value of your home may decline by far more than the cost of maintenance. If you don't replace a bad car in order to avoid buying a newer one, you may lose income or even your job because you couldn't make it into work because of breakdowns.

If you don't invest in the tools of your trade (the most important being your brain), you run the risk of losing promotions or even losing your job to those better equipped to do it.

The key to financial success and security is in the wise use of resources, not in their mere retention.

Waste is worse than loss. The time is coming when every person who lays claim to ability will keep the question of waste before him constantly.

Thomas A. Edison (1847-1931)
Inventor, Businessman

Economy is too late at the bottom of the purse.

Seneca (54 BC-39 AD)
Roman Statesman

Doing more with less is the mantra of both businesses and individuals today. Competition within the business world forces organizations to constantly look at the way they do business and look for ways to increase outputs and/or reduce inputs. Households don't face such competition, but they don't have the same ability to increase revenues that businesses do. Increasing revenues in a household is a long-term proposition that requires more education, relocation, or other steps that don't happen overnight. Decreasing and prioritizing expenses is one of the few short-term tools available to a household to improve efficiency.

The single biggest reason why so many people fail to reach their financial goals is because they never set any. The first step to any financial success is to set a goal that can be measured. Any such goal needs to be measurable in both time and dollars. For example, people often set a target date for retirement, but don't complete the goal by setting an amount. You may say you want to retire at sixty-two, but unless you know how much money it will take to retire at that age, you can't begin to take the steps necessary to reach that goal.

> *Plan ahead: it wasn't raining*
> *when Noah built the ark.*
>
> Richard Cushing (1895-1970)
> Archbishop of Boston
>
> *A goal without a plan is just a wish.*
>
> Antoine de Saint-Exupery (1900-1944)
> French Writer

Once a goal has been quantified with a date and an amount, it is necessary to create a plan to get from here to there. Most people can set a date for such goals, but determining an amount is more difficult, and formulating a plan to get there is beyond the skill set of all but a few. Certified Financial Planners are trained to help people formulate realistic goals and devise and implement a plan to get them where they want to go.

> *The man who is prepared has his battle half fought.*
>
> Miguel de Cervantes (1547-1616)
> Spanish Novelist, Poet

> *By failing to prepare you are preparing to fail.*
> Benjamin Franklin (1706-1790)
> Founding Father

Most of our financial goals are long-term goals. Short of winning a lottery or receiving an unexpected inheritance, there is no way to seriously compress the time frame needed to reach those long-term goals. If someone needs to save for twenty years to fund ten years of retirement, they can't start at fifty and retire at sixty, unless they are certain they will be dead by sixty-five. If they start at fifty and they are expected to live to eighty-five (a reasonable assumption), they would have to work until seventy-four in order to save enough to retire. Every day of delay in starting a plan creates a day of delay in meeting a goal.

Plans should not be static, either. In the 1990's, when the stock market was climbing 20% year in and year out, people were planning for retirement assuming similar returns would continue indefinitely. The first decade of the twenty-first century blew a serious hole in those plans, and those who haven't adapted by increasing savings or delaying the starting date for retirement will find retirement something to be dreaded instead of anticipated.

There will always be external forces that will affect your financial plans, and very few of those forces will affect them positively. It is a common trait to be overly optimistic when considering possible outcomes. We think this way because we want the best outcome to prevail, and so we make the best outcome the most likely outcome in our calculations. Unfortunately, the world doesn't often cooperate - inflation spikes, markets crash, pensions disappear, promotions evaporate, and Junior is still living at home when he's in his thirties.

Few people even bother to calculate how much they will need to save for retirement, even though that is the most critical financial obligation they will have in their lifetimes. Retirement planning involves some calculation of your income needs in retirement, which is based on expected number of years in retirement, expected income needs, plus a calculation for inflation both prior to and during retirement. It's a daunting task, and one reason most people don't do this type of planning is they know on some level that what they are currently doing is inadequate. Denial may be comforting now, but the discomfort later isn't worth it.

> *A man with a surplus can control circumstances, but a man without a surplus is controlled by them, and often he has no opportunity to exercise judgment.*
>
> Harvey Firestone (1868-1938)
> Founder, Firestone Tire Company

If you've ever tried selling a car on your own, you have probably encountered the prospect who makes a lowball offer and has cash to buy the car on the spot. If you were not pressed financially at that moment and if you knew the car were worth more than what was being offered, you could afford to decline the offer. However, if you needed cash right away to avoid some financial calamity, you may have had no choice but to sell your property for far less than its true value. The cause of this one-sided deal was a surplus of cash by one party and a dearth of it by the other. The party with the ready cash controlled the circumstances and, therefore, the terms of the deal. The buyer could walk away more easily than the seller could.

> *The man least indebted to tomorrow*
> *meets tomorrow most cheerfully.*
>
> Epicurus (341-270 BC)
> Greek Philosopher
>
> *Annual income twenty pounds, annual expenditure nineteen six, result happiness.*
> *Annual income twenty pounds, annual expenditure twenty pounds ought and six, result misery.*
>
> Charles Dickens (1812-1870)
> English Novelist

The difference between surplus and deficit may not be big, but it will always be significant. The difference between a five percent surplus and a five percent deficit is only ten percent of income. In many cases a ten percent change in income may not cause major changes. However, if it turns a deficit into a surplus, or vice versa, it can be the difference between prosperity and insolvency. The distance between the windward and leeward side of a mountain may only be a few yards, but which side a seed lands on determines if it will dissolve into soil or become a mighty tree.

> *The rich rule over the poor*
> *and the borrower becomes the lender's slave.*
> Proverbs 22:7
>
> *Debt is the worst poverty.*
> Thomas Fuller (1608-1661)
> English Writer, Historian

Until the sixteenth century, the church forbade the charging of interest on a loan. Previously, the charging of any interest was considered usury, which we define today as the charging of excessive interest (the definition of excessive varies). The reason for the ban on charging interest was the belief that only a person in dire financial straits would seek out a loan; further, to take advantage of a person in that situation for personal profit was considered a sin. Naturally, if interest could not be charged, loans were made for altruistic reasons only, which meant there was little borrowing or lending before the sixteenth century.

As our understanding of finance increased, we realized that there could be profit in borrowing money, so it was only right that there should be profit in lending money, too. Borrowing was almost always limited to the financing of a business enterprise, whether it was a loan for a farmer to buy seed or a blacksmith getting a loan to build a new forge.

The profit incentive also greatly increased the funds available to be loaned. Once it became possible to make money with money alone, banking soon developed. Banks brought borrowers and lenders together in an orderly manner.

Only in the last century has borrowing occurred at the consumer level. A combination of new products for the home and the individual, plus demand generated by advertising, combined with more sophisticated techniques by retailers, including the financing of purchases, created the debt-fueled consumer culture we take for granted today.

Back in the first half of the twentieth century, credit was given by individual businesses to customers, without any third parties. The creation of the Diner's Club Card in 1951 enabled a single charge account to buy items from many different businesses. Diner's Club was a charge card, not a credit card, which meant the balance had to be paid in full at the end of each month. Credit cards, as we know them today, were introduced in 1959. With a credit card, the balance did not have to be paid in full, although interest charges would accrue.

The ability to accumulate large amounts of unsecured debt has led to financial disaster for millions of households over the last fifty years. As credit card debt became more acceptable, so did greater debt on secured loans, like cars and homes. Large loan amounts were often limited because of the size of the monthly payment. Lenders overcame that obstacle by increasing the period of time to repay the loan. In the 1950's, the maximum repayment period on a car loan was twenty-four months; today it is eighty-four. Back then, the maximum repayment period on a home loan was twenty years; today it is thirty.

Longer repayment periods have increased the

debt load of households because consumers focus on the monthly payment, not on the amount borrowed. The creation of interest-only loans with adjustable rates has enabled borrowers to borrow more while paying less each month. Such loans seem like a good deal until interest rates rise and the time comes to begin repaying principal. Then it all begins to fall apart for the consumer.

The largest single item of debt for most households is their home, which is nothing new. However, the process by which many homeowners obtained their mortgage is very different from times past.

> *To preserve our independence, we must not*
> *let our rules load us with perpetual debt.*
> *We must make our election between*
> *economy and liberty, or profusion and servitude.*
>
> Thomas Jefferson (1743-1826)
> 3rd U.S. President
>
> *It is difficult to set bounds to the price*
> *unless you first set bounds to the wish.*
>
> Cicero (106-43 BC)
> Roman Statesman

In the twentieth century, mortgages originated from, and were held by, the local banks. There were strict underwriting standards because the bank was loaning the money of its depositors, and any default had to be absorbed by that bank alone. Naturally, they were cautious in their lending.

More recently, mortgages were not held by the people who originated them. They were sold, resold, bundled together with similar mortgages, cut into pieces called tranches, and sold to investors who were looking for high-yielding "safe" investments. The demand for these investments brought in a flood of money for lenders to lend. As a result, lenders were more than eager to lend almost any amount to almost anybody. There were large fees to be made, and the loan originators assumed no risk in the event of default - that had been shifted to those investors who bought these new investments, known as **collateralized debt obligations** (CDOs).

Naturally, many of the loans that were made were not being repaid as agreed. When the defaults began to mount up, the value of all of these CDOs began to crash. The total value of these CDOs was in the trillions, and Wall Street firms, major banks, insurance companies, pension funds, even governments were holding huge amounts of these things. It was the collapse in value of these allegedly safe investments that led to the near total collapse of the world economy in 2008.

It seems crazy that the entire world economy could have imploded because people, mostly in America, were buying more home than they could afford. However, what happens on a macro level is simply a magnification of what is happening on a micro level. If an abnormally high percentage of American households were defaulting on their mortgages, the damage should be limited to those households. Because of the increasingly complex and interconnected financial markets, people all over the world can pay the price for bad financial decisions made in just a small percentage of

American homes. Bad decisions and risky behavior can infect even those who pay their debts on time and who never knowingly take undue risks.

> *Good times are when people make debts to pay in bad times.*
>
> Robert Quillen (1887-1948)
> Journalist, Humorist

When all this money was being pumped into the mortgage market by investors looking for higher yields with low risk, it naturally created a bubble in housing prices. Prices are based on supply and demand, and demand is based on how much money is available to pursue the supply. Because housing prices were on a steady climb, people were refinancing their homes to pull out the equity to spend on cars, vacations, college tuition, even second homes.

Many borrowers used interest-only, adjustable-rate mortgages to get into their dream home. Even though they knew that there would be an interest rate increase in the future and that there would be a balloon payment as well, they looked at the price appreciation statistics and calculated that by the time those events occurred, the value of their home would have increased enough that they could tap the increased equity and just keep going.

> *Statistics are no substitute for judgment.*
>
> Henry Clay (1777-1852)
> Member, U.S. Senate

All these new homes needed to be furnished, so other debt, especially credit card debt, also soared during this period. The one thing that wasn't soaring during this period was household income, which was keeping up with inflation, but nothing more. The monthly debt service was creating a cash flow crisis in households across America.

The final straw occurred when housing prices not only stopped increasing, but began a steep decline. For those people who had bought at the top of the market, made no down payment, had an interest rate hike and/or a balloon payment coming up, and who also owed twenty or thirty percent more than the house was now worth, the solution was simple - walk away.

> *The sound of your hammer at five in the morning,*
> *or eight at night, heard by a creditor,*
> *makes him easy six months longer.*
>
> Benjamin Franklin (1706-1790)
> Founding Father

The relative ease with which so many people defaulted on their mortgages was a shock to the financial system and nearly destroyed it. Looking back at the situation though, the reaction of these homeowners was about the only logical act in the whole tragedy.

If someone has none of his/her own hard-earned money in an investment, if the monthly debt service has increased to the point where it is impossible to cover it, and if the penalty for defaulting is nothing more than a damaged credit history (no more debtor's prisons), it is perfectly logical to default. Personal bankruptcies also shot up during this period. The stigma of bankruptcy has largely disappeared, and even if it were still there, for many it was preferable to drowning under a tsunami of debt.

> *Neither a borrower nor a lender be*
> *For loan oft loses both itself and friend,*
> *And borrowing dulls the edge of husbandry.*
>
> William Shakespeare (1564-1616)
> English Playwright

The personal debt accumulated by Americans in recent years, and their inability to pay back much of it, has rocked financial markets. What has gone largely unseen is what the borrowing has done to families and friends who were lenders. Many of the homes that were foreclosed on were purchased with money borrowed from relatives to cover down payments or closing costs. When people began feeling the full weight of their debt, and the usual lenders were no longer amenable, they turned to friends and relatives to bail them out. Whether the requests were granted or not, the request itself was sure to put a strain on the relationship. At a time when family and friends were needed for moral support, the relationship was suffering because of financial support either given or denied.

> *Do not be among those who give pledges, who become guarantors for debts. If you have nothing with which to pay, why should he take your bed from under you?*
>
> Proverbs 22:26-27
>
> *An acquaintance is someone we know well enough to borrow from, but not well enough to lend to.*
>
> Ambrose Bierce (1842-1913)
> Journalist, Satirist

Personal loans were one thing, but many friends and relatives cosigned for loans during this period. When the cosigner became responsible for the debt and they didn't have the resources to pay, they saw their own good credit ruined. If someone makes a personal loan, all that is at risk is the amount of the loan. Cosigning a loan can be far more costly than simply lending that person the money directly; although, if someone needs a cosigner, that's a good sign of a bad credit risk.

> *If you owe the bank $100, that's your problem. If you owe the bank $100 million, that's the bank's problem.*
>
> J. Paul Getty (1892-1976)
> Founder, Getty Oil Company

If average American borrowers had been aware of how lending had changed in recent years, they would not have been so willing to defer to the judgment of the lenders as to their own credit-worthiness. Many borrowers assumed that, if the banks were willing to loan them the money, then they shouldn't worry about their own ability to repay it. What the borrowers didn't realize was that the banks were merely processing a loan for a fee. Their interest was in making the loan and selling it, not in making sure it was a good loan to make. Had the average borrower recognized that the bankers were now operating like car salesmen, they might have been a little more skeptical about accepting the banker's word that this loan was what they needed and that repaying it would be easy.

> *For which of you, intending to build a tower, does not sit down first and count the cost, whether he may have enough to finish it; lest perhaps, after he has laid the foundation and is not able to finish, all those seeing begin to mock him, saying, This man began to build and was not able to finish.*
>
> Luke 14:28-30

One of the tragedies of the debt-fueled housing bubble and bust of the 2000's was the long-term damage that so many families have incurred. Part of the American dream is to own your own home. The government, along with organizations like Fannie Mae, attempted to increase homeownership. While their intentions may have been noble, they ended up doing a great disservice to those they intended to serve. Homeownership is a big responsibility. First, there is a mortgage that is likely the single biggest monthly expense, and it continues in most cases for thirty years. Then there are property taxes and homeowners insurance to be paid. There is also the obligation to maintain the property.

There are financial costs to maintenance that can be both high and unpredictable. There is the unstated requirement that the homeowner devote personal time and effort in the home's upkeep. Maintenance is necessary to protect the investment, but also to protect the integrity of the neighborhood and good relations with the neighbors. Many people who bought homes during the boom years saw only the upside; by the time they fully saw the downside, it was too late.

> *There is no dignity quite so impressive*
> *and no independence quite so important*
> *as living within your means.*
>
> Calvin Coolidge (1872-1933)
> 30th U.S. President
>
> *More people should learn to tell their dollars where to go instead of asking them where they went.*
>
> Roger W. Babson (1875-1967)
> Founder, Babson College

If wisdom is learned through suffering, then Americans and much of the world should be much wiser now than they were at the beginning of the millennium. For those who still have time to rebuild their assets, they are likely to take a more disciplined approach, recognizing that the behavior of the investor is more important than the behavior of the investment.

Human behavior tends to swing like a pendulum, though. Those who assumed too much risk and got burned in recent years are likely to become too risk averse. They may become so conservative that they will be unable to reach their long-term goals. They are like the golfer who, after slicing the first tee shot off to the right, overcompensates by hooking the next one off to the left.

Here is an example of how being too conservative can be costly. A new college graduate begins work and starts saving for retirement. If that person is conservative and earns only a 4% return on contributions over the next forty years, the contributions will grow by about 140%. If the return is 7%, the same contributions will grow by almost 400%. The balance at the end of forty years is more than double if the return is 7% instead of 4%.

> *All man's gains are the fruit of venturing.*
>
> Herodotus (484-425 BC)
> Greek Historian

There is no way to skate around the economic axiom that risk and reward move in the same direction. The shenanigans of Wall Street in recent years were due in large part to attempts to socialize the risk while privatizing the profit. There will always be people trying to game the system, which is why strong regulation and enforcement will always be needed.

For the average citizen-investor, the reward they get will be commensurate with the risk they are willing to assume. After recognizing this fact, the first mistake that often gets made is misjudging one's own tolerance for risk. When everything is going well, we don't tend to see risk when it exists, and we become too risk tolerant. When everything is going badly, we swing like a pendulum in the other direction, becoming too risk averse and over-estimating the real dangers out there.

Many, if not most people get the risk-reward relationship wrong. They think that the risk they need to assume is based on the reward they are seeking. They see the reward as fixed and their tolerance for risk as flexible. In truth, the reward you get is based on the risk you can tolerate; the risk you tolerate isn't based on the reward you seek.

Consider the self-employed business owner. Most of the millionaires in the U.S. are members of this class. Most people look at the income, wealth, and freedom that this class of people has, and everyone would like the same for themselves. What doesn't get taken into account is the enormous risks that these successful businessmen and women took to create a successful business. What also isn't seen are the corpses of all the businesses that failed while the successful ones were fighting for survival. People want the rewards of owning a successful business; they just don't want the risks. If people could adjust their risk tolerance to match their desired reward, there would be millions more small businesses being created every year.

> *Big shots are only little shots who keep shooting.*
>
> Christopher Morley (1890-1957)
> Novelist, Journalist

> *Whenever you see a successful business, someone once made a courageous decision.*
>
> Peter Drucker (1909-2005)
> Management Consultant

Relatively few people venture out and start their own business, and fewer still ever reach a level of success that makes the rest of us jealous. The traits that make someone successful in creating a business are also needed for someone successful in the world of investing - courage, faith, patience, knowledge.

> *Nothing tells in the long run like a good judgment, and no sound judgment can remain with the man whose mind is disturbed by the mercurial changes of the stock exchange. It places him under an influence akin to intoxication. What is not, he sees, and what he sees, is not.*
>
> Andrew Carnegie (1835-1919)
> Founder, U.S. Steel Corporation

With the exception of a few celebrities, no one can expect to get rich from one's own labors. Wealth is created when you enable some of your money to go out into the world and reproduce with abandon. Money, like people, cannot reproduce without taking on a certain amount of risk.

Investments that are truly risk-free will earn, at most, enough interest to keep even with inflation. In other words, if you invested $1,000 in something that merely kept up with inflation, you could buy the same item in forty years that you could have bought for $1,000 today, with nothing left over. You would have gained nothing; you would have postponed the use of that item for forty years, however.

Most people will work for about forty years. Hopefully, during that entire time they will be contributing to a retirement plan. If they will be retired for twenty years (a modest expectation) and if their "safe" investments only return enough to offset inflation, those people would need to save **one-half** of their incomes over their forty year working life to adequately fund retirement; no one can be expected to do that.

Over the last forty years the S&P 500 has increased thirteen fold (excluding dividends), despite all the economic and political turmoil during that period. If the S&P 500 outpaces the inflation rate by 4% per year on average, investing in the S&P 500 would require saving only **one-fifth** of one's income over a forty-year working life. Since employers typically make some contribution as well, the worker's required savings rate would be reduced by the employer's contributions.

Anyone can hold the helm when the sea is calm.

Publilius Syrus (1st Century BC)
Latin Writer

No one would have crossed the ocean if he could have gotten off the ship in the storm.

Charles F. Kettering (1876-1958)
Inventor, Businessman

When it comes to investing, the seas will never

be as calm as they were in the past. The reason is we keep churning them up.

In the old days, a person's retirement fund was managed by professional money managers, who made the investment decisions regarding the pension fund. The employee had neither responsibility nor input as to the management of the fund. Because the management was left in the hands of people who were not emotionally attached to the money, they could behave rationally regarding investment decisions. As a result, performance was adequate to fund the company's pension obligations.

When the traditional pension was replaced with the 401(k) plan, the investment decisions were shifted to the employee. This shift was bad for two reasons. First, the average employee could not hope to know a fraction of what the professionals knew about investment management. Second, even with adequate knowledge, the emotional attachment to the money being managed meant that the average employee would react to short-term market movements, rather than remain focused on the long-term. It also didn't help that they could check on their 401(k)'s every morning when they logged on to their computers.

People have a tendency to take what has happened in the recent past and extrapolate it out into the indefinite future. If the last three months have been bad in the stock market, many people think the trend will continue for the next three decades and pull their money out of stocks. For these people, they find themselves sitting on the sidelines when the inevitable rebound occurs. Once they are certain the bear market is over, they get back in, which is usually somewhere close to the end of the bull market. They then manage to ride the next down cycle before panicking again and selling. They are participating in the market, but only during the bad times.

> *The stock market is a giant distraction from the business of investing.*
>
> John C. Bogle (1929-)
> Founder, Vanguard Group
>
> *In the short run, the market is a voting machine. But in the long run, it is a weighing machine.*
>
> Ben Graham (1894-1976)
> Economist, Investor

Because information is available to everyone instantly at little or no cost now, there is no advantage to frequent trading, or even moves in and out of the market altogether. If everyone has access to the same information, the price of any investment will already have that piece of information factored in before you or anyone else can act to take advantage of it.

> *We believe that according the name 'investors' to institutions that trade actively is like calling someone who repeatedly engages in one-night stands a 'romantic.'*
>
> Warren Buffett (1930-)
> Investor, Philanthropist

It is certainly possible to "beat the market," though that phrase is something of a misnomer. In order to beat the market, you merely have to be more disciplined than the herd. On good news, most people will buy; on bad news, they will sell. In most cases, the person who is really making money is the person on the other end of those trades.

Going back to a variation on the pendulum analogy, if someone is swerving from pessimism to optimism with every market gyration, they are swerving to the right and then the left, when their destination is straight ahead. If your destination is ten, twenty, thirty, or forty years into the future, will the movements of the market in a single day, week, or even a month have any impact on arriving at your destination on time? Unless you can travel forward in time to know with certainty what the markets will do in the near-term, focusing on the near-term is a waste of time.

The big money is not in the buying or the selling, but in the waiting.

Jesse Livermore (1877-1940)
Stock Speculator

The intelligent investor is a realist who sells to optimists and buys from pessimists.

Ben Graham (1894-1976)
Economist, Investor

When events are unfolding rapidly, and especially when markets are being affected, the natural instinct is to want to "do something." There is a bias toward action. However, time and time again it has been proven that, when everything and everyone seem to be going crazy, maintaining self-discipline and, if action is warranted, responding rather than reacting, are the keys to winning. Whatever the majority is doing is almost always the least profitable course of action.

> *One of the funny things about the stock market is that every time one man buys, another sells, and they both think they are astute.*
>
> William Feather (1889-1981)
> Publisher, Author
>
> *The market, like the Lord, helps those who help themselves. But unlike the Lord, the market does not forgive those who know not what they do.*
>
> Warren Buffett (1930-)
> Investor, Philanthropist

Part of the frustration of investing is the knowledge that you could have always done something better. It doesn't matter if you have beaten the market and all of your peers in the investment arena. As long as some money was left on the table, it is hard to be completely satisfied. Also, as long as we are not completely satisfied, there will be the temptation to do something more. Giving in to that temptation, however, is likely to leave us even less satisfied when our actions work against us.

Speaking of the investment arena, it isn't one. An arena is a place where competition takes place and where there are winners and losers. Investing is not a competitive sport. Your job is to focus on meeting your goals, which do not include beating anyone else. If your brother-in-law is bragging about his great investment returns, ignore him. His results have no effect on your results, and besides, he's probably lying.

> *In order to understand the stock market, we have to realize that, like anything enormous and inert, it's fundamentally stable, and like anything emotion-driven, it's volatile as hell.*
>
> P.J. O'Rourke (1947-)
> Satirist, Journalist

As long as we remember that investment markets were designed by, are run by, and exist to serve human beings, it is easier to accept all the human quirks and faults that manifest themselves in those markets. In the short-term, people may drive us crazy, but we don't give up on the whole lot and become hermits. We accept them with all their faults and recognize that we're better off with them than without them. So it is with the markets as well.

> *I distrust men or concerns that rise up with the speed of rockets. Sudden rises are sometimes followed by equally sudden falls. I have most faith in the individual or enterprise that advances step by step. A mushroom can spring up in a day; an oak takes fifty years to mature. Mushrooms don't last; oaks do.*
>
> B.C. Forbes (1880-1954)
> Founder, Forbes Magazine

> *Time is the friend of the wonderful company, the enemy of the mediocre.*
>
> Warren Buffett (1930-)
> Investor, Philanthropist
>
> *Never invest your money in anything that eats or needs repairing.*
>
> Billy Rose (1899-1966)
> Showman, Lyricist

The three determinants of investment success are **investment selection, asset allocation**, and **investor behavior.** Investment selection involves picking the specific stocks, bonds, etc. that make up the investment portfolio. Asset allocation involves deciding what percentage of a portfolio will be in stocks, bonds, etc. Asset allocation is where the risk in a portfolio is measured.

Investor behavior is everything the investor does in setting up a portfolio and managing it afterward. Investment selection can be affected by the investor's proclivity to trade versus buy-and-hold. Asset allocation can be affected by whether the investor is aggressive or conservative.

Studies that looked at how these three pieces contribute to investment success had some surprising results. Investment selection had an effect of about 5%; asset allocation had an effect of about 15%; investor behavior had an effect of about 80%.

What do these findings mean? The specific stocks, bonds, etc. that you select has only a minimal impact on your returns. Much more important is the asset allocation. Over the long run, it's less important what stocks you own than to simply own stocks.

By far, the single most important factor in investment success is the human factor, aka, investor behavior. If you sell a stock when it's temporarily down, you hurt yourself. If you buy and sell frequently, you hurt yourself. If you are too aggressive for your tolerance or too conservative for your goals, you hurt yourself. If you get too hot when things are hot and too cold when things are cold, you hurt yourself. If you follow the herd instead of marching steadily to your own destination, you hurt yourself. When it comes to investing, we are usually our own worst enemy.

> *Retirement at sixty-five is ridiculous.*
> *When I was sixty-five I still had pimples.*
>
> George Burns (1896-1996)
> Comedian

When the Social Security Act was passed in 1935, the retirement date was set at age sixty-five. At that time, half the workers eligible for Social Security never lived to sixty-five, and the other half lived an average of only five years after retirement. In the early years of Social Security, ten workers paid into the system for every person who collected benefits.

Today, there are five workers paying into the system for every two people collecting benefits. The earliest age to begin receiving benefits has dropped from sixty-five to sixty-two. These changes have occurred over a period when the average life expectancy of Americans has increased by nearly twenty years.

Social Security was created to be a safety net for the elderly in the midst of the Great Depression. It was also created to entice older workers into retirement, which would enable younger workers to find jobs and thus lower the unemployment rate. Social Security was never meant to be the primary source of retirement income.

If sixty is the new forty, then why are people clamoring to retire at ever earlier ages? If sixty is the new forty, it is due largely to the extra years that medical advances have provided to us. If the average American worker now lives at least fifteen years longer than his/her counterpart from the 1930's, is it unrealistic to expect that worker to spend at least half of those bonus years at work?

How old would you be if you didn't know how old you are?

Satchel Paige (1906-1982)
Baseball Player

The question isn't at what age I want to retire, it's at what income.

George Foreman (1949-)
World Boxing Champion

Retirement is not an entitlement, at least not a retirement that encompasses a quarter or more of one's life and is funded largely by others. Everyone who lives to a normal life expectancy and retires at the normal retirement age will collect more in Social

Security benefits than they ever paid in, even after accounting for inflation.

The failure of Social Security to increase the qualifying age for benefits as our lifespans have increased not only jeopardizes the integrity of the entire system, it also sends the wrong message to millions of Americans. Because we have been told from the day we first went to work that it is normal to retire at or around sixty-five, we have spent our entire adult lives aiming to do just that. As a result, people have focused more on getting to retirement age than finding a career from which they would never want to retire. Additionally, some of the best workers leave the workforce prematurely, simply because they've been trained to believe that's what they are supposed to do at a certain age.

There are certainly jobs that become difficult, if not impossible, to do beyond a certain age. Those jobs, however, make up a much smaller percentage of the economy than they did in 1935. Our current retirement system makes no consideration for the ease or difficulty of certain jobs for older workers. An insurance actuary can collect Social Security benefits at the same age as a construction worker, even though one job is clearly much easier for a sixty-year-old to do than the other.

The few jobs that still offer traditional pensions have also not changed with the times. Many jobs with pensions are in the public service sector, as businesses have moved from defined benefit to defined contribution retirement plans. To qualify for these pensions, one typically has to work for thirty years or have a combination of age and years on the job that totals eighty-five. These requirements mean that a person who begins a job at age twenty-five can retire with full benefits at age fifty-five. Most of these jobs offer some cost-of-living increases, too. Since these workers may live another thirty years in many cases, they stand to collect more in pension payments than they ever received in pay.

Most people retire while they are still productive workers. Many go into retirement unsure about what they will do, as well as having doubts about the financial viability of retirement. Leaving a job that provides a sense of purpose as well as financial stability for the uncertainties of retirement is often the result of societal pressure, not choice.

> *Retirement kills more people than hard work ever did.*
>
> Malcolm Forbes (1919-1990)
> Publisher, Forbes Magazine

Many retirees, especially those who retire artificially early, often find themselves struggling financially after a few years. By then though, they may not be in good enough health to return to work. They may also not have the up-to-date skills that would be needed to return to work. It would be better to retire with security at sixty-seven than to retire at sixty-two, only to find yourself struggling at seventy-two with another decade or more to live.

More people are transitioning into retirement, rather than going from full-time work to full-time nothing in one step. They typically retire from a full-time job, but then work part-time doing something of interest to them. This intermediate stage helps them make their two most difficult adjustments: they begin living on a smaller income, and they begin to fill hours that were previously spent on the job.

> *Don't think of retiring from the world*
> *until the world will be sorry that you retire.*
> Samuel Johnson (1709-1784)
> English Poet, Essayist

Current retirees generally have three sources of income: Social Security, pensions, and personal savings. The luckiest have all three. Future retirees should count on only one source of retirement income - their own personal savings.

Social Security is likely to be around in some form for the foreseeable future, but demographics and economics will force it to provide an ever-smaller percentage of a retiree's income. Even those jobs that currently provide a traditional pension at retirement can't be counted on to provide that pension when the time comes. Such plans have no ceiling on costs for the employer, which means that employers will continue to do away with them and replace them with defined contribution plans, which we know as the 401(k).

The problem with saving for retirement with a 401(k) plan is that the best time to invest in the plan is when you are so young that retirement is almost unimaginable. If you are twenty-five, you can't picture yourself at sixty-five. If you can't picture yourself at sixty-five, you aren't going to defer current spending to fund a 401(k). With retirement plans that mandatorily deducted contributions from the employee's paycheck, or that were funded totally by the employer, funding was not a problem. Today, the employee has to make the decision to defer income now to be invested into the 401(k).

> *Cessation of work is not accompanied by cessation of expenses.*
>
> Cato the Elder (234-149 BC)
> Roman Statesman

The shifting of retirement funding from the employer (pension) to the employee (401(k)) has meant that the determining factor of when a worker retires is no longer age or years of service; it is the balance in the 401(k).

As much as someone may want to retire at sixty-five (or sixty-two or fifty-five), age and years of service will not be a factor. In order to retire today, people will need to have a sufficient amount in their retirement and other accounts.

What is a sufficient amount? It varies with the individual, but here is a general guideline. If someone retires around age sixty-five, he/she should plan to be around for at least twenty years. For a withdrawal period of that length, it is prudent not to withdraw more than five percent of the balance in the first year. That guideline means that you would need **twenty times** your first year's withdrawal in your 401(k) on the day you retire. If someone anticipated needing $50,000 from the account the first year, they should have a starting balance of $1 million.

This situation assumes a "normal" retirement age and an investment portfolio that isn't overly conservative. If someone wants to retire at sixty and if he/she only wants "safe" investments, at least **thirty times** the first year withdrawal will be needed to maintain solvency through a normal retirement.

> *A man is not old until regrets take the place of dreams.*
>
> John Barrymore (1882-1942)
> Actor
>
> *Growing old is not for sissies.*
>
> Bette Davis (1908-1989)
> Actress

Most people working today, even those close to retirement, are unaware of what it will take to live with some semblance of dignity and independence in retirement. If they did, many might just give up and not even bother saving for retirement, thinking that it was a lost cause. Living in denial does not change the facts, though. Even if these people think that they will just keep on working, almost everyone reaches the stage in life where they can no longer work, regardless of whether they need the income.

Hopefully, those who choose to live in denial would make up a small minority of the population. For the rest, the solution is two-fold: invest more now and expect to work longer. Increasing contributions to the 401(k) plan works best for younger workers - the older we are, the less time there is for the contributions to grow. Working longer helps in two ways - every year of working enables more contributions to be made to the 401(k). In addition, every year of work is a year that is not spent in retirement, drawing down precious capital.

Even if most of us have to work into our seventies, our working lives are better than those of our grandparents. Even our retirement is likely to be both longer and better than that of our grandparents, if we each accept our responsibility to make it so.

BRIGHTER REFLECTIONS

We expect money to bring out the worst in people. It also has the ability to bring out the best.

When people look for labels to describe our many good and bad behaviors, they will often refer to our "lower natures" or our "higher natures." When considering human behavior as it relates to money, greed would epitomize our lower nature, while generosity epitomizes our higher nature.

These labels are more accurate than one might think. The **nucleus accumbens** is one of the oldest and most primitive parts of the human brain. It is sometimes referred to as the pleasure center. The highs that are experienced from sex, drugs, gambling, and other addictions all originate in the nucleus accumbens. The highs that come from acquisition and accumulation, the manifestations of greed, also originate there. The nucleus accumbens is the biological source of some our worst behavior when it comes to money.

There is a different part of our brain that can take credit for our best behavior regarding money. The **posterior superior temporal sulcus** (PSTC for short) resides at the top of our brain. The PSTC takes care of our social calendar and all our human relationships. All development as a human society is the result of the PSTC. It is the part of the brain that most separates human beings from animals. The PSTC is also where our generosity resides.

> *And He sat down opposite the treasury, and began observing how the people were putting money into the treasury; and many rich people were putting in large sums. A poor widow came and put in two small copper coins, which amounts to a cent. Calling His disciples to Him, He said to them, "Truly I say to you, this poor widow put in more than all the contributors to the treasury; for they all put in out of their surplus, but she, out of her poverty, put in all she owned, all she had to live on."*
>
> Mark 12:41-44

Brain studies have shown that the nucleus accumbens and the posterior superior temporal sulcus cannot function simultaneously; when one is active, the other goes dormant. We can be greedy or we can be generous, but we cannot be both, at least not simultaneously.

The nucleus accumbens has an unfair advantage in this competition. It produces dopamine, the chemical that can make anything and everything feel good to us. Addictive behavior is the result of dopamine being released when we engage in certain activities. Greed can be an addictive behavior if it produces large amounts of dopamine. In truth, what humans become addicted to is dopamine, and we will undertake any activity that will produce it in sufficient quantities, even harmful and antisocial behavior.

Money giving is a very good criterion, in a way,
of a person's mental health.
Generous people are rarely mentally ill people.
Dr. Karl Menninger (1893-1990)
Psychiatrist

Our impulse to be generous operates on a much higher level. We possess no instinctive desire to be generous. Small children provide evidence that generosity must be taught, but that selfishness is inherent. Despite the unfair competition, how does generosity manage to manifest itself in a sizable portion of mankind?

Sigmund Freud defined three main parts of our psychiatric apparatus - the **id**, the **ego**, and the **superego**. The id is all about seeking pleasure and avoiding pain. The id is about I-me-mine. Freud called the id, "the dark inaccessible part of our personality...a cauldron full of seething excitations." The nucleus accumbens is the physical address for greed and selfishness; the id is their psychological address.

The ego represents our common sense, and it spends its days trying to find a happy medium between the id and the superego.

The superego is where our conscience resides. The superego is the psychological manifestation of the PSTC. If the id represents our lower nature, the superego represents our higher nature. If we are generous, it is because the superego has gained the upper hand over the id and has given the PSTC a chance to show that it can provide experiences that, if not exactly pleasurable, are certainly rewarding.

We make a living by what we get;
we make a life by what we give.
Winston Churchill (1874-1965)
British Prime Minister

Leave the woodpile higher than you found it.
Paul Harvey (1918-2009)
Broadcaster

Because of money's versatility, how people deal with money may be the best indicator of whether the id or the superego is in control.

People have been saying that time is money ever since money was first invented over 2,500 years ago. When it comes to generosity, giving money has been used as a substitute for giving time for just as long. For many givers, time is a more precious resource than money, so giving money is the easier sacrifice. For many receivers, money provides the flexibility to buy the time of others to meet their needs. If you cannot provide your time directly to help others, your money may prove just as useful to them.

People have also been saying that money can't buy love for at least 2,500 years. Money can actually be one of the best tools ever invented for the **expression** of love. However, it is one of the worst tools ever as a **substitute** for love.

There are times when only your time and only your love are acceptable to others. The most obvious example is in your relationship with your children. Children need the time and love of their parents, and no amount of wealth can substitute for them. The closer your relationship is with any individual or group, the less you can use a gift of money as a proxy for the gift of yourself.

> *We do not quite forgive a giver. The hand that feeds us is in some danger of being bitten.*
>
> Ralph Waldo Emerson (1803-1882)
> Philosopher, Essayist

When you are generous, whether it is with your time or your money, there is always the chance that your generosity will not be appreciated. One reason that people may bite the hand that feeds them is that they resent the need to be fed. If you need to rely on others to be fed, you may feel like a failure, or at least inferior to someone who has a surplus to offer to you. Their resentment may be at themselves or at the circumstances that created their current situation, but the convenient target of that resentment is often the person who is trying to help.

When there is a lack of appreciation by the recipients of generosity, there is a natural tendency to want to withdraw support and find more "worthy" recipients. Before making such a move, it may help to try to view things from the perspective of the "ungrateful" recipient. Everyone needs his/her dignity and self-respect and charity can strip those away. For those who seem unreceptive to a handout, what they may really need is a hand up. A hand up may require more than a handout, but the results will almost always be better. The recipient can maintain his/her dignity and will be less likely to require a handout in the future.

> *For where your treasure is, there your heart will be also.*
> Luke 12:34
>
> *We can tell our values by looking at our checkbook stubs.*
> Gloria Steinem (1934-)
> Feminist, Journalist

Which comes first, the money or the commitment? Most people would say that the money follows the commitment, which makes sense on first review. If you believe in a cause, you are more willing to devote time and money to it. It certainly makes it easier to write a check if you agree with the goals of an organization.

Jesus took a different approach. He believed that if you committed your money to something, you would then commit yourself, too. Two examples will serve to illustrate.

Children are sent to private schools with the expectation that they will receive a superior education than they would receive at public school. To insure that they get what they are paying for, the parents of children in private school devote much more time and effort (as well as money) in supporting the mission of the school. If their children are receiving a superior education at private school, it is due primarily to the level of involvement of the parents, rather than the quality of the teachers.

The housing collapse that led to the financial

crisis has been studied in depth. Many causes have been considered, and much data has been collected. There is one statistic that stands out, though. Regardless of geography, demography, or any other classification, there was one constant - the lower the down payment on a house, the higher the incidence of default. When people had their own money sunk into their home, they were much more likely to do everything in their power to keep it their home. In both of these examples, the financial commitment created an emotional bond, not the reverse.

> *Never measure your generosity by what you give, but rather by what you have left.*
>
> Fulton J. Sheen (1895-1975)
> Archbishop of New York
>
> *Make all you can, save all you can, give all you can.*
>
> John Wesley (1703-1791)
> English Cleric

Altruistic intentions can be a great motivator to create wealth. When personal wealth reaches the point where a person can fulfill every material desire, the only motivation to continue creating wealth is to give it away. The motivation may be as personal as funding a college education for grandchildren, or it may be as grand as creating an endowment that provides scholarships in perpetuity. In addition to motivating wealth creators to continue creating wealth, altruism helps assure that the methods used to create wealth meet the highest ethical standards. Few people want to help one group of people with money that was obtained by harming another group of people.

> *Work for your future as if you are going to live forever, for your afterlife as if you are going to die tomorrow.*
> Arabian Proverb

One of the great motivations for philanthropy, altruism, charity, generosity, whatever you label it, is the desire to leave a legacy of some sort. Older people give at higher levels than younger people. This tendency prevails even when incomes and expenses favor the younger group. The older we get, the more we recognize our own mortality. As we realize that our time is becoming more and more limited, the desire to do something that will live beyond us becomes stronger.

We can give in one of three ways - time, talent, or treasure. Not everyone has talents that translate into benefits for others in need. Time always seems to be in short supply, and even if there is the time, there is usually the need for some talent to go along with the time.

Treasure can be the most useful gift for several reasons. First, money is fungible - it can be mixed with other money without changing any of the money's characteristics. Second, money has an indefinite useful life. Time that is given to a cause is gone immediately. Talent may produce something of more permanence, but even cathedrals decay over time. Finally, money is flexible. Money that is given to a good cause today might not be spent for fifty years. In fifty years' time, that money might be used to supply a product or fill a need that the donor could not have imagined a half-century before.

> *Someone is sitting in the shade today because someone planted a tree a long time ago.*
>
> Warren Buffett (1930-)
> Investor, Philanthropist

Despite money's many qualities, including its ability to be transported to the future, one quality it does not possess is the ability to be taken with us when we die. When people realize they can't take it with them, they begin to think of ways to maintain some control of their money from the beyond. The less they trust their beneficiaries to do the right thing with an inheritance, the more restrictive and ironclad the trusts will be that control the estate.

Estate laws are so complex that attorneys can spend their entire careers in that one specialty. As long as wealth can be accumulated, but can't be taken into the next world, and as long as those who remain behind may fight over and squander an inheritance, there will be a need for trusts to carry out the wishes of the person who created the wealth.

> *Study the past if you would divine the future.*
>
> Confucius (551-479 BC)
> Chinese Philosopher

When beneficiaries of a trust complain about the restrictions of the trust, they probably don't stop to think that there was a reason those restrictions were put in place. If the deceased had simply wanted to be mean, the best thing would have been to leave the beneficiary nothing at all. A person who is the beneficiary of a restrictive trust must face two facts - the dear departed cared enough to make that person a beneficiary, and the beneficiary had not behaved in a manner to earn complete trust.

> *The excesses of our youth are drafts upon our old age.*
>
> Charles Caleb Colton (1780-1832)
> English Cleric, Writer
>
> *Many people take no care of their money till they come nearly to the end of it, and others do just the same with their time.*
>
> Johann Wolfgang von Goethe (1749-1832)
> German Writer, Philosopher

When most people hear the word **stewardship,** they think of the annual pledge drive at their church. Stewardship is actually the careful and responsible management of something entrusted to one's care. To accept the role of steward is to first accept that, although we might possess something, it doesn't mean we own it.

In a country like the United States, with our emphasis on individual property rights, it can be difficult to accept that we are merely stewards of what we legally own. However, we have all known people who lost what they legally owned through neglect or carelessness or abuse. Whether you consider it a law of economics, of nature, or of God, a prerequisite to getting more is taking care of that which is already possessed.

> *Those who make the worst use of their time most complain of its shortness.*
>
> Jean de la Bruyere (1645-1696)
> French Essayist, Moralist

Time is the most valuable resource because the proper use of time is the source of all wealth. Unless a person is a good steward of his/her time, it is impossible to be a good steward of anything else. Considering the amount of time the average American spends watching TV and surfing the internet, a strong case can be made that, as a nation, we are not good stewards of our time.

In addition to wasting the present time, too many of us are depleting our reserves of time. Medical advances may be adding years to our lives, but we reduce both the quality and quantity of our future time by not taking proper care of ourselves.

Some believe that we have only so many heartbeats in our lifetime, and they don't want to waste them exercising. However, if an hour of exercise each day lowered a person's resting heart rate from seventy-two to sixty, that person would gain four hours of heartbeats per day, even after allowing for the extra beats used exercising. The essence of good stewardship is taking care of what you have today to enable having more in the future.

> *The future is purchased by the present.*
> Samuel Johnson (1709-1784)
> English Poet, Essayist
>
> *It is better to have a hen tomorrow than an egg today.*
> Thomas Fuller (1608-1661)
> English Author, Historian

Just as we should allocate our money between sharing, saving, and spending, we should do the same with our time. Even if we are good at making such allocations with money, we often avoid doing so with our time. This avoidance may result from a feeling of no control over our time. It may also result from the uncertainty of how much time we have. Money, which is measurable with great accuracy, does not suffer such uncertainties.

We don't need to know how much time we have left to begin allocating it. We all have twenty-four hours each day. Those twenty-four hours should be allocated between sharing (doing something to help others), saving (doing something to make your future better), and spending (living in the moment). If we take care of each day in this manner, the future, no matter how much of it we have, will become better.

> *The cost of a thing is that amount of life*
> *which must be exchanged for it.*
> Henry David Thoreau (1817-1862)
> Author, Philosopher

There is a big difference between living **in** the moment and living **for** the moment. Living in the moment means you get everything the present has to offer. Living for the moment means you see nothing but the present. Living in the moment makes the future better without compromising the present. Living for the moment sacrifices the future for the pleasures of the present.

By the street of By-and-By,
one arrives at the house of Never.

Miguel de Cervantes (1547-1616)
Spanish Novelist, Poet

You can't escape the responsibility of tomorrow
by evading it today.

Abraham Lincoln (1809-1965)
16th U.S. President

We know about the price of procrastination when it comes to saving for retirement, but we don't often think about how procrastination affects our future in less measurable ways. Procrastination is defined as needless delay. The definition should be broadened to say that procrastination is needed action needlessly delayed. It is only the delay of needed action that has consequences. If you don't get a haircut this week, neither you nor the world is likely to suffer. If you don't have needed surgery this week, you and the world are likely to suffer as a result.

Most of us are aware, on some level, of the consequences of our procrastination. Even if we can't fully comprehend the consequences on our own, there is rarely a shortage of family and friends who are imploring us to take needed action now to avoid some future disaster. Procrastination does not occur unintentionally; it involves knowingly doing nothing with full knowledge that the price to be paid in the future is higher than the price to be paid today.

> *Cause and effect, means and ends, seed and fruit cannot be severed; for the effect already blooms in the cause, the end preexists in the means, the fruit in the seed.*
>
> Ralph Waldo Emerson (1803-1882)
> Philosopher, Essayist

While no one can predict the future, we all have a power even more awesome - the ability to affect the future. Because we can each affect our future, for better or worse, there is no need for predictive powers. In exchange for these powers, we are charged with accepting responsibility for that which we can change for the better, but choose not to. For example, none of us knows when we will die, and few of us would really want to know. We do have the power to affect that date by lifestyle choices we make every day. On this matter, I much prefer the ability to affect the outcome than to predict it.

> *The afternoon knows what the morning never suspected.*
> Swedish Proverb

We will never be able to affect everything to the extent we would like. Part of unpredictability is not knowing how much of an effect our efforts will have on a future outcome. In addition, many of the major events in our life come at us out of deep left field. There is nothing to be done about them. We can only deal with what we know might happen. If we focus on those matters of higher probability, we will be in a better position to deal with the occasional matter that blindsides us.

> *Don't worry 'bout the mule goin' blind -*
> *just keep loadin' the wagon.*
>
> Appalachian Proverb

When a large part of the world was freed from the yoke of communism toward the end of the last century, they were faced with a new problem. In their longing for greater opportunities, average people never realized that they would now become more responsible for their own fates. Communism had provided a cradle-to-grave floor and ceiling for these people. Unfortunately, the ceiling was just inches above the floor. They were glad to be rid of the ceiling, but they had to lose the floor as well. Some soared, but many crashed.

> *When one door closes another door opens; but we often look so long and so regretfully upon the closed door that we do not see the ones which open for us.*
>
> Alexander Graham Bell (1847-1922)
> Scientist, Inventor

It is amazing how focused and productive people can become when they are under the pressure of a deadline. Part of this productivity can be explained in relative terms - they are productive near the deadline in comparison to their procrastination when the deadline was in the distant future. Even people who are consistently productive manage to find another gear when it becomes necessary. If everyone were consistently as productive at work as they are right before they leave on vacation, there would be no economic problems in this country.

> *It is not half as important to burn the midnight oil as it is to be awake in the daytime.*
>
> E. W. Elmore

Many people argue that they "work best under pressure." The pressure of a deadline may kick start them into working harder, but "working best" is hardly the same thing as doing one's best work. Ask any college professor who has ever graded term papers. The papers that have been assembled consistently throughout the semester always outshine the ones that were assembled in a panicked state in the last forty-eight hours before the deadline. The only point of pride the procrastinating student can claim is that they were very productive for the small amount of time and effort they expended on the project, which is not really something to brag about.

> *Forty is the old age of youth.*
> *Fifty is the youth of old age.*
>
> Victor Hugo (1802-1885)
> French Poet, Novelist

> *If it is sensible for the child to make an effort to learn how to be an adult, then it is essential for the adult to learn how to be aged.*
>
> Alfred Stieglitz (1864-1946)
> Photographer

There is a reason why advertisers prefer to sponsor TV shows that have high ratings in the 18-34 age bracket. They prefer this age group over the 50-and-older age group even though the second group has much more disposable income. Why do advertisers go after the younger audience? Simply put, the younger the audience, the more gullible they are.

Most of us get wiser with age. We may decline in most other aspects once we pass fifty, but if we've been paying attention to the world at all, we should be accumulating no small amount of wisdom by that age. Wisdom is the combination of experiences and the willingness to learn from those experiences. Both ingredients are essential, which is why there are few wise young people and why there can still be foolish old people.

Old people who have cultivated and harvested wisdom throughout their lives rarely regret getting old. They see their physical decline as a small price to pay for their increased insight. Those who have learned little over the decades, but have merely grown old, are those seniors you see who can find no comfort in their advancing years. A wise senior is a happy senior. We should appreciate the wisdom of this group and try to learn all we can from them.

> *If all our misfortunes were laid in one common heap, whence everyone must take an equal portion, most people would be content to take their own and depart.*
> Socrates (469-399 BC)
> Greek Philosopher

All of us have uttered the idiom, "Better the devil you know" at some point. Invoking that phrase is an admission that, while we may not always be treated fairly, we also realize we could be treated even more unfairly, and it is risky to tempt the fates.

One manifestation of wisdom is the ability to recognize that we rarely have control over outcomes. We do, however, have control over inputs, which are the main determinants of outcomes. Too many people go through life under the delusion that their inputs will have no effect on outcomes, that it is all controlled by others, the fates, or the stars.

> *Life is like a game of cards. The hand that is dealt you represents determinism; the way you play it is free will.*
> Jawaharlal Nehru (1889-1964)
> Indian Prime Minister

How is it that some people are born into poverty and become captains of industry, while others are born into wealth and privilege and become broken and destitute? While such cases often involve some lucky and unlucky breaks, the real determinant is how the characters played the cards they were dealt.

If you've ever ridden a ten-speed bicycle, you

know that you work very hard and don't go very fast when you are in the lower gears. That situation is similar to people who are born with no inherent advantages and have to struggle to cover any ground. You also know that once you work your way up to tenth gear, you cover ground quickly with relatively little effort. That situation is similar to people who are born to great advantage, who are in effect placed at birth on a bicycle that is already moving at a high speed. Someone who is placed on a bicycle travelling at speed may have an initial advantage, but they also haven't worked their way through the gears, and that lack of experience and perspective can make them a greater risk to crash.

> *Good and bad luck is a synonym, in the great majority of instances, for good and bad judgment.*
>
> John Chatfield (1826-1863)
> Colonel, Union Army
>
> *Lots of folks confuse bad management with destiny.*
>
> Elbert Hubbard (1856-1915)
> Writer, Philosopher

"I'm a victim of coicumstance!" When Curly of The Three Stooges used to utter that phrase, it was hilarious. It's not hilarious today, when so many people say it in total seriousness. Victim mentality has become rampant in recent years, as every misfortune borne must have an accountable party, and yet that party is never the person who was the recipient of the misfortune.

The most successful people are those who

recognize that misfortune is a part of life and that there are some misfortunes that are unavoidable. These people also recognize that it makes no sense to try to control uncontrollable circumstances. They devote their energy to responding positively to events and looking to turn a disadvantage into an advantage. They look for ways to make the best of a bad situation, rather than looking for someone to blame for the bad situation.

It never occurs to fools that merit and good fortune are closely united.

Johann Wolfgang von Goethe (1749-1832)
German Writer, Philosopher

Where no plan is laid, where the disposal of time is surrendered merely to the chance of incident, chaos will soon reign.

Victor Hugo (1802-1885)
French Poet, Novelist

Successful people have an obsession about moving forward. Progress, more than profits, are their driving force. To that end, they do not leave the course of their journey to chance. They plan meticulously, while maintaining flexibility to adapt to changing conditions along the way. They also see any misfortune as a learning opportunity. They do not adopt a victim mentality; quite the opposite. They will look closely at any misfortune to see what **they** did wrong, in order to learn from the experience and avoid similar mistakes in the future.

> *'Tis known by perseverance in a good cause,*
> *and obstinacy in a bad one.*
>
> Laurence Sterne (1713-1768)
> Anglo-Irish Clergyman

Successful people also have the ability to discern when effort reaches a point of diminishing returns. They are known as **satisficers,** rather than **maximizers.** Maximizers will stick with something until it is perfected which, if it ever occurs, may take so much effort to get there that it isn't worth it. Satisficers work until they are satisfied, and then move on to another project. They are typically satisfied when they recognize their time and efforts can yield more progress if spent elsewhere. While the quest for perfection may seem noble, it is almost never practical. Successful people are nothing if not practical.

> *Failure can be bought on easy terms;*
> *success must be paid for in advance.*
>
> Cullen Hightower (1923-)
> Writer

Successful people not only know when to stop working on a project, they know when to start, too. All success is the result of initiative, the willingness to get started on something without being forced to. Those with initiative are successful because they understand that, until they get on the bike and start pedaling, they will never be able to cruise in high gear.

Failures are divided into two classes –
those who thought and never did,
and those who did and never thought.
John Charles Salak

Have you ever seriously considered the command "Ready, Aim, Fire!"? They are three simple instructions, all of which must be followed in the proper sequence to offer any chance for success. Some people never even bother to get ready. Some people will get ready and aim, but never muster the courage to fire. Worst of all are those who amend the sequence to "Ready, Fire, Aim!" They are the worst because they expend energy and resources wastefully and, because they fire before they aim, they risk doing more harm than good by their actions. Their haste makes waste and sometimes worse.

Everyone who has ever played golf knows the agony of flubbing a shot because, in the rush to look up and see a great shot, the head came up too soon, guaranteeing the duffer wouldn't like the results. Nothing hurts the chances for a good result like being in too big a rush to see that result. There will always be time to admire a great result, but it will come only by remaining focused on the task while the task is still being performed.

It is the mark of a good action that
it appears inevitable in retrospect.
Robert Louis Stevenson (1850-1894)
Scottish Novelist

Successful people are less likely to lose focus while working on a task because they are good at visualizing the results. They know what a good result looks like, and they know how to create that result. Because they remain "in the moment" when they are working on something, they can look back with pride when they finish. Rare is the person who can combine a sense of vision with the discipline and ability to successfully execute that vision.

> *Manners often make fortunes.*
>
> John Ray (1627-1705)
> English Naturalist
>
> *Civility costs nothing and buys everything.*
>
> Mary Wortley Montagu (1689-1762)
> English Aristocrat, Writer

When we think of people who are disciplined and successful, there is also a tendency to think of them as domineering, overbearing, even bullies. While some certainly fit that description, the most successful do not. They understand that you do not get the best work from people by employing such tactics. They also understand that such tactics create enemies, not allies.

One look at popular culture will confirm that we are far less civil than in the past. This decline in civility is actually an advantage for those who can show consideration for others. The bar is now set so low for personal behavior that it is easy to stand out as someone who knows how to treat others properly. Such a person never lacks for business opportunities.

> *Wealth, like happiness, is never attained when sought after directly. It comes as a by-product of providing a useful service.*
>
> Henry Ford (1863-1947)
> Founder, Ford Motor Company
>
> *Success is not the key to happiness.*
> *Happiness is the key to success.*
>
> Albert Schweitzer (1875-1965)
> German Theologian, Physician

Of all the great accomplishments of our Founding Fathers, perhaps none is greater than the inclusion of our right to "the pursuit of happiness" in the Declaration of Independence. No government had ever been founded on such a vague concept, and there were certainly guffaws in the Parliament when that passage was first read. The British must have thought us mad to risk annihilation over such a trivial desire. Still, there were some there who marveled at the audacity of it all, and they knew that a people who believed that happiness was a right would not be easy to defeat.

Although we value our right to pursue happiness, we often don't have a good understanding of what happiness is or how to achieve it. One of the most common mistakes we make is confusing pleasure with happiness. Pleasure is typically sensual in nature and involves receiving rather than giving. Happiness is more emotional and involves giving more than receiving. Pleasures can be bought, but they do not last, and the pursuit of them often impedes the opportunities for happiness in the future.

> *All earthly delights are sweeter in expectation than enjoyment; but all spiritual pleasures more in fruition than expectation.*
>
> Owen Feltham (1602-1668)
> English Essayist

Because money can buy things that can give us pleasure and because we tend to confuse pleasure with happiness, we then believe that money will make us happy or that it can buy happiness.

Studies have shown that there is only a slight correlation between wealth and happiness. People at low income levels are less happy, which is due in large part to the daily struggle to meet basic needs. However, disparities in income do not translate to similar disparities in happiness. The middle class is only slightly happier than the lower class, and the upper class is barely any happier than the middle class. A severe lack of money can make someone unhappy, but an abundance of money will not make someone happy.

> *Not everything that can be counted counts.*
> *And not everything that counts can be counted.*
>
> Albert Einstein (1879-1955)
> Theoretical physicist

Each of us have our own idea and interpretation of happiness. Because we can choose what makes us happy, we do not have to get extravagant in what we do to become happy. Most people agree that true happiness comes from actions that lead to self-fulfillment or in actions that help others. Happiness can come from learning a new skill or from teaching someone else a new skill. Money may be a useful tool in the creation of happiness, but it is hardly an essential ingredient.

> *For what does it profit a man to gain the whole world, and forfeit his soul?*
>
> Mark 8:36
>
> *The trouble with the rat race is, even if you win, you're still a rat.*
>
> Lily Tomlin (1939-)
> Actress, Comedian

Misunderstanding the relationship between success and happiness, as well as misunderstanding the difference between the two, has led to a lot of disappointment over the centuries. To begin with, many people think that, if they become successful, happiness will follow, just as night follows day. They never stop to define what happiness means to them, so they never know what they are seeking. They expect that happiness will simply appear and that they will know instinctively when it has arrived.

While these people don't define what happiness means to them, they usually create some definition of success for themselves. Success is typically defined by them through position or money, with the main purpose of position being to provide a lot of money. Because money is the primary measurement of success, it also is expected to bring happiness in proportion to its amount. As studies have shown, more money does not lead to more happiness, so the people who thought that more money leads to more happiness inevitably find themselves disappointed and still looking for a source of happiness.

The tragedy for many of these people is the extent to which they compromised their principles to achieve financial success. Many merely allowed relationships to suffer because their attention was elsewhere. Many hurt their own physical and emotional health by obsessing over money. Some went to the extreme of breaking the law to get what they wanted. When their goals were achieved, they realized too late that the prize was not worth the price.

To be without some of the things you want is an indispensible part of happiness.

Bertrand Russell (1872-1970)
English Philosopher

There are three ingredients in the good life: learning, earning and yearning.

Christopher Morley (1890-1957)
Novelist, Journalist

We should all take time to carefully calculate the cost-benefit balance before we undertake any attempt at success and happiness. Such analysis can be difficult, however, because it is too easy to miscalculate the benefit side of the equation. If the cost becomes higher than we originally estimated, we will compensate by increasing our perception of the benefit. One of the biggest problems with this type of cost-benefit analysis is the inability to know the true value of the benefit until it has been obtained. By then, all the costs have been incurred and if the benefit doesn't live up to expectations, there can be a lot of disappointment.

Despite the difficulties in accurately estimating the level of happiness one can expect from various endeavors, we should never stop looking for new challenges. Once people achieve financial success and find it to be less rewarding than expected, they can begin to look for new challenges that don't involve material gain for personal benefit. They may look to challenges of a physical, mental, or spiritual nature, such as running a marathon, earning a degree, or studying a new religion. They may also continue with financial challenges, but with a different twist. They may become fundraisers or philanthropists for causes close to their heart. Achieving a goal in any of these categories is likely to bring greater happiness than any personal financial accomplishment they may have achieved.

> *Hope itself is a species of happiness, and, perhaps, the chief happiness which this world affords; but, like all other pleasures immoderately enjoyed, the excesses of hope must be expiated by pain.*
>
> Samuel Johnson (1709-1784)
> English Poet, Essayist

An optimist is a product of faith combined with hope. Pessimists can be a necessary counterweight to a world full of optimists, but the optimists keep the world moving forward. Even though optimists are the drivers of progress and even though hope is a key ingredient to optimism, there needs to be an element of realism as well. Realism can make the optimists more flexible, allowing them to maintain their optimistic nature even when events turn out badly.

> *Hope is a good breakfast, but it is a bad supper.*
> Francis Bacon (1561-1626)
> English Philosopher, Statesman
>
> *He that lives upon hope will die fasting.*
> Benjamin Franklin (1706-1790)
> Founding Father

One of the great characteristics of America and Americans is our optimistic nature, even during hard times. We have this personality as a nation because we are a place where hope continues to spring anew. Because opportunities for the individual are more unlimited here than anywhere else, there is always a high measure of hope among the population. As long as our citizens feel confident that they have a reasonable chance of realizing their dreams, hope will remain high.

America is like spring training in baseball. The slate has been wiped clean, and every team feels they have a shot at the championship this year. By August your team may be out of it, but even then you can console yourself that there is always next year. However, if the team owner and managers never take steps to convert hope into victories, the fans will eventually run out of hope. Hope cannot be refilled unless it is at least occasionally fulfilled.

> *Everything that is done in the world is done by hope. No merchant or tradesman would set himself to work if he did not hope to reap benefit thereby.*
>
> Martin Luther (1483-1546)
> Founder, Protestant Reformation

A pessimist is, by nature, someone devoid of hope. No enterprise, much less a successful one, was ever started by a pessimist. Even those who bet against the market hope their predictions will be correct. They are optimistic that they can profit from the pessimism of others during such periods. To my knowledge, no one ever started a business with the slogan, "This isn't gonna work." If anyone did, I'm sure they were proven right in short order.

As previously stated, risk and reward move in the same direction. To generate greater rewards requires the assumption of greater risks. No one takes on risk, especially higher levels of risk, unless there is the hope that the risks will be managed and the rewards will be reaped.

> *We must dream of an aristocracy of achievement arising out of a democracy of opportunity.*
>
> Thomas Jefferson (1743-1826)
> 3rd U.S. President

It shouldn't be surprising that America is a nation of (mostly) optimists. As a nation of immigrants, we were populated by people who came to the U.S. with the hope of building a better life. If there were any pessimists on the boat coming over, they either became optimists once they got settled, or they eventually became discouraged and returned to the old country.

> *There is no sadder sight than a young pessimist.*
> Mark Twain (1835-1910)
> Author, Humorist

Young people are similar to immigrants in that they are new to the workforce and have a long future ahead of them. Like most immigrants, they are starting at the bottom of the ladder and will have to work their way up.

If young people lose hope for their future, America's future is in serious jeopardy. If they feel that their inheritance will be nothing more than trillions of dollars of debt, they will lose hope, and we will quickly become a nation of pessimists. A nation of pessimists is a doomed nation. Perhaps the most important duty of any citizen is the building of a foundation of hope for the next generation. Each generation has the responsibility to make their own achievements, but each generation also has the responsibility to create for the next generation as many opportunities as they themselves enjoy.

> *Hope is independent of the apparatus of logic.*
> Norman Cousins (1915-1990)
> Journalist, Author

It can be tempting to think that honesty and integrity impede profitability. Unfortunately, in the short term, that is often the case. One of the problems of the current system of compensation for corporate executives is the emphasis on bonuses for short term results. Those who think only in the short term will be more likely to compromise their principles to improve their financial position. As a result, unethical and often illegal methods are used to boost profitability and generate executive bonuses. Such methods may work for a brief period, but eventually the truth comes out when the schemes collapse under their own weight.

The superior man seeks what is right;
the inferior man, what is profitable.

Confucius (551-479 BC)
Chinese Philosopher

If honesty did not exist, we ought to invent it
as the best means of getting rich.

Honore De Mirabeau (1749-1791)
French Revolutionary

The overwhelming majority of businesses are run by honest, ethical, hardworking people. In the short run, they will be at a disadvantage to competitors who are not honest and ethical. Eventually, the unethical are discovered for what they are, if not by the law then by their customers. Once the discovery is made, it is only a matter of time before they are put out of business. Unfortunately, there will always be some new competitor looking to cut corners.

> *He who is faithful in a very little thing is faithful also in much; and he who is unrighteous in a very little thing is unrighteous also in much.*
>
> Luke 16:10

Integrity cannot be compartmentalized. When evaluating the behavior of leaders, whether they are in the public or the private sector, it is tempting to claim that their private behavior should not affect our opinion of their job performance. That attitude might be appropriate for someone who has no position of leadership. However, leading isn't what someone **does**; a leader is who someone **is.** A leader is always a leader, even when not executing the duties of leadership. Leaders are not allowed the luxury of compartmentalizing their lives. Any unethical behavior affects every aspect of their lives, most especially their ability to lead.

> *I would rather have people laugh at my economies than weep for my extravagance.*
>
> Oscar II (1829-1907)
> King of Sweden

Inevitably, when someone with questionable ethics moves into a leadership position, those ethics surface in the execution of duties. It is folly to think that a person with a poor history of personal financial management will do any better with the company's finances. It is folly to think that a person who has been unfaithful to a spouse will be faithful to the shareholders and employees. It is folly to think that a person who has always put his/her interests above those of others would act any differently when put in a position to act in even greater self-interest.

Few men have virtue to withstand the highest bidder.

George Washington (1732-1799)
1st U.S. President

No one worth possessing can be quite possessed.

Sara Teasdale (1884-1933)
Poet

Personal integrity and technical competence are not mutually exclusive. In fact, integrity is the foundation upon which competence is built. Personal integrity involves setting standards of behavior that are not subject to negotiation. People who unilaterally set high expectations for their personal behavior will also set similarly high expectations for their job performance. Conversely, people who do not hold themselves accountable for their personal behavior cannot be expected to act any differently on the job.

The best way to become a respected leader and reap financial rewards is to first demand a standard of behavior of yourself that makes you worthy of such position and wealth.

COUNTERPOINT

Loosening the screws on the current crop of humanity

When we were young, at some point, we all had to endure some old geezer complaining, "When I was your age...," followed by some rant about how his/her generation endured more/complained less, worked harder/played less, gave more/took less, and especially about how they were so much better behaved than our present generation.

Every generation is shaped by the circumstances of their times. If the people who grew up in the Great Depression were exceptionally frugal, it was because they had no money. The armies that won World War II knew that living under Nazi rule would be worse than death itself. History shows that the human race responds to circumstances as it needs to in order to survive.

Our relative physical comfort today is not the result of laziness; it is actually the result of hard work and imagination. Air conditioning, microwaves, automobiles, and countless other inventions have enabled us to channel our energies into new and more productive efforts. One of the main reasons that women are now the majority of the workforce is because inventions of the twentieth century greatly reduced the amount of time and effort it took to perform the tasks of maintaining a home. Women work as hard as they ever did; they have simply been relieved of some of the hard work their predecessors performed.

We have become too fat in recent years, which is the first time in history where widespread obesity has even been possible. The poorest state in the U.S., Mississippi, also has the highest obesity rate, which would have been an unimaginable phenomenon just a few decades ago. Hunger around the world today is largely the result of political conflicts, not food shortages.

Dr. Norman Borlaug died in 2009 at the age of ninety-five. He was a recipient of the Nobel Peace Prize, the Congressional Gold Medal, and the Presidential Medal of Freedom. You probably never heard of him, even though he is credited with saving over **one billion** people to date.

Dr. Borlaug is considered the founder of the Green Revolution, which refers to the series of scientific advances in agriculture that greatly increased crop yields. Dr. Borlaug's work over a period of more than sixty years enabled the number of hungry people in the world to decline even as the population of the world was tripling. In 1968, Dr. Paul Ehrlich wrote *The Population Bomb*, which predicted wars and other devastation over the fight for food to feed an ever-increasing population. The book speculated that we might not even make it to the twenty-first century. Dr. Ehrlich's work has been discredited because of the work of Dr. Borlaug and others. The Green Revolution is an example of how the human race rises to meet challenges when they must be met. If obesity is our major health problem, there isn't a person from the past who wouldn't exchange obesity for the major health problem of his/her own era: pneumonia, typhus, smallpox, tuberculosis, polio, cholera, diarrhea, bronchitis, influenza, malnutrition - the list of candidates was quite long. Most of these killers aren't even on our radar screen anymore.

There is one factor that determines the economic success or failure of a people more than anything else, and it is a factor we don't often consider. The single greatest determinant of economic success is the type of government a society establishes.

One need only look at the difference between North and South Korea or the difference between East and West Germany before reunification to see that places that initially differ only in their form of government can end up with very different economic conditions. These differences are evident even within a single country. China has become an economic power because its government, while still very controlling, has scrapped the old communist model for a more free market approach to growth.

Free countries are rich countries. In 1950, only about 43% of the world's population lived in democracies. Today that figure is approaching 70%, despite the fact that population growth is still highest in countries that are not democracies. The Middle East, one of the last bastions of totalitarianism, is currently undergoing an enlightenment by the people that they will continue to fall behind if they allow these dictators and monarchs to remain in power. They are using the example of the U.S. and other democracies as inspiration for their demands for change. Such reforms can rarely be imposed from the outside, but they can be very successful if they are produced by the citizenry of a nation.

Democracy has spread to many nations; it has also spread more evenly within nations. We have been a democracy for nearly a quarter of a millennium, but only in the last half-century have many of our citizens become fully enfranchised. In less than a lifetime, African-Americans, women, gays, and many other groups who were previously denied a full share of the American dream are now part of the mainstream. This progress required the majority of Americans to think differently than their parents and grandparents thought. As much as any generation before, Americans today want to do what is right, even if it isn't easy.

The furor over global warming has obscured an important fact - the environment is in better shape today than it has been since the early days of the Industrial Revolution. There will be challenges going forward as more of the world enjoys more material prosperity, but the environment has never been as protected as it is today.

The automobile of today emits less than 5% of the pollutants of its 1970 counterpart. That figure will continue to improve as hybrids and electric cars become more common. Fuel economy has vastly improved, even as engines have become more powerful. Cars are safer than ever before. Even though the total miles driven have more than tripled since 1950, the number of annual auto fatalities in the U.S. is lower today. We go farther, faster, on less fuel, and with less pollution than ever before.

If electric power were the great invention that enabled the growth of the twentieth century, the microchip is the great invention for the twenty-first century. The microchip and the powerful computers it has spawned will change the way we live more than any invention since the wheel. We have only begun to scratch the surface of what we can do with this still-young technology. Most of the solutions to the problems we face today will involve computer technology in some way. The existence of the microchip and the solutions it can provide also means that we will be able to solve more of our problems in the future than we ever could in the past. It is no longer a question of **if** we can solve our biggest problems; it is only a question of **when.**

The average American household annually donates about five percent of its income to charities. While this percentage has held fairly steady over time, it can be somewhat deceptive. Over the years, the percentage of tax revenues that are allocated to help the disadvantaged has increased significantly. As a result, the average American family today gives more to help others than previous generations did. Despite the fact that much of that giving is non-discretionary in the form of taxes, discretionary giving has held steady as a percentage of income. Instantaneous communication has also enabled the population as a whole to be more informed about people in need, as well as being able to contribute immediately through online giving and electronic transfers.

We operate in a closed system. When I say "we," I am referring to Planet Earth. A closed system means there is nothing that comes from, or goes to, anything outside the system. Because we operate in a closed system, we are responsible for everything that happens within that system. If we damage the environment, we can't blame anyone but ourselves. If we declare war on each other, we can't blame anyone but ourselves. If we spend ourselves into financial ruin, we can't blame anyone but ourselves.

Many of the illustrious figures I've quoted in this book would disparage us for our alleged financial malfeasance. Much of their criticism would be justified. Never in history has a population had such abundance, and yet were willing to risk destroying the financial system that made this abundance possible, merely to have more sooner, rather than later.

Some of these illustrious figures would recognize that we are as human today as they and their peers were. We suffer the same temptations, weaknesses, and stupidity that have plagued mankind since our inception. They might lament our lack of progress, but they would understand that, if their peers were placed in our position, they would have probably gotten into the same predicaments.

I believe that virtually all of these great minds would reserve final judgment to see how we address the problems we have made for ourselves. They would be most impressed if we can recognize our folly for what it is and take steps to change before we create a full-blown crisis. They would be significantly less impressed if it took a full-blown crisis of our own making to galvanize us into actions that would have been less painful if we had been more proactive and less reactive.

Finally, I believe that every one of these founts of financial wisdom would justifiably condemn us, should we neglect our responsibilities to ourselves and our posterity and allow our financial recklessness to destroy a system that created wealth that they could have never imagined. If we choose such a course of action, "swine" is too good a word for us.

INDEX OF QUOTATIONS

Mark DiGiovanni is a Certified Financial Planner with more than a quarter-century in the profession. In addition to creating and running a successful financial advisory firm in Atlanta, Mark is a recognized author, speaker, and teacher on how we can attain and maintain financial success without sacrificing those things that money can't buy.

More information about Mark is available at
www.mark-digiovanni.com

Books by Mark DiGiovanni

Made in the USA
Charleston, SC
11 August 2011